W9-BZX-974

GREAT MINDS OF SCIENCE

Ernest Rutherford

Father of Nuclear Science

Naomi Pasachoff

Enslow Publishers, Inc.

40 Industrial Road   PO Box 38
Box 398   Aldershot
Berkeley Heights, NJ 07922   Hants GU12 6BP
USA   UK

http://www.enslow.com

Dedication:
For Eloise, Tom, and Deborah

Library of Congress Cataloging-in-Publication Data

Pasachoff, Naomi E.
 Ernest Rutherford : father of nuclear science / Naomi Pasachoff.
   p. cm. — (Great minds of science)
 Includes bibliographical references and index.
 ISBN 0-7660-2441-5
 1. Rutherford, Ernest, 1871–1937—Juvenile literature. 2. Nuclear
physicists—New Zealand—Biography—Juvenile literature. 3. Physicists—
New Zealand—Biography—Juvenile literature. 4. Nuclear
physics—History—Juvenile literature. I. Title. II. Series.
 QC16.R8P37 2005
 539.7'092—dc22

                                   2004013402

Printed in the United States of America

10 9 8 7 6 5 4 3 2 1

To Our Readers:
We have done our best to make sure all Internet Addresses in this book were
active and appropriate when we went to press. However, the author and the
publisher have no control over and assume no liability for the material
available on those Internet sites or on other Web sites they may link to. Any
comments or suggestions can be sent by e-mail to comments@enslow.com or
to the address on the back cover.

Illustration Credits: AIP Emilio Segrè Visual Archives (Gift of Otto
Hahn and Lawrence Badash), p. 67; Cawthron Institute, Nelson, New
Zealand, courtesy AIP Emilio Segrè Visual Archives, p. 98; courtesy of
Jay M. Pasachoff, pp. 53, 69; Enslow Publishers, Inc., pp. 17, 77, 80,
83; Nature, courtesy AIP Emilio Segrè Visual Archives, p. 102; photo-
graph by D. Schoenberg, courtesy AIP Emilio Segrè Visual Archives
(Bainbridge Collection), p. 39; photograph by Mark Oliphant, cour-
tesy AIP Emilio Segrè Visual Archives, Margrethe Bohr Collection, p.
86; U.K. Atomic Energy Authority, courtesy AIP Emilio Segrè Visual
Archives, p. 12.

Cover Illustration: Science Photo Library (background); Nature,
courtesy AIP Emilio Segrè Visual Archives (inset).

Contents

Acknowledgments

I would like to thank those individuals who assisted me in preparing this book. My husband, Professor Jay M. Pasachoff of the astronomy department at Williams College, helped me understand the fine points of Rutherford's research, read various drafts of the manuscript, and took many photographs related to Rutherford, two of which appear in these pages. I have enjoyed his company on visits to Cambridge, Montreal, Manchester, and Copenhagen, where I was able to deepen my understanding of different periods in Rutherford's career. I am grateful to Professors Tommy Mark and Jean Barrette of the Department of Physics at McGill University for arranging a private tour for my husband and me through the small Rutherford Museum there in summer 2003.

I am lucky enough to have friends in New Zealand who live near Rutherford's birthplace in Nelson. John and Mary Glaisyer, the parents of our son-in-law, Tom Glaisyer, were kind enough to take photographs of the birthplace and to bring a crisp $100 New Zealand bill with Rutherford's picture on it to our daughter's wedding to their son.

Also in New Zealand, John Campbell, a physicist at the University of Canterbury and himself a biographer of Rutherford, read and commented on the final draft of the book.

At Williams College, physicist William K. Wootters, assisted me in defining the difference between a theoretical physicist and an experimental physicist.

If any errors have crept into these pages despite the intervention of these individuals, I take full responsibility for them.

As always, I am deeply grateful to members of my family for their support during the course of my career in general and of this project in particular: my mother, Anna J. Schwartz, a researcher for over sixty years at the National Bureau of Economic Research, who at 89 is working on another major contribution to economic history; my sister, Paula Berggren, professor of English at Baruch College of the City University of New York; my daughters Eloise, a recent graduate of the Kennedy School of Government and of Harvard Law School, and Deborah, now a graduate student at the Sloan School of Management at the Massachusetts Institute of Technology; and my son-in-law, Tom Glaisyer, now a graduate student at the School of International and Public Affairs at Columbia University. Their commitment to their respective undertakings, as well as their empathy for the angst every author sometimes feels, have nourished me over the years.

A Scholarship He Almost Did Not Win

IN JULY 1895 A YOUNG MAN, NOT YET twenty-four, was working in the potato fields on his parents' farm in New Zealand. He was justly proud of the original scientific research that had recently resulted in three academic degrees from the University of New Zealand. When he was back home, however, he was still expected to do his share of chores.

He had received as good an education as New Zealand could then offer, but the recent graduate knew he would have to go abroad to become a truly great scientist. He needed financial aid to support that goal, however. In 1894 the University of New Zealand had a chance to secure a prestigious scholarship for one of its science graduates. The scholarship enabled graduates of universities throughout the British Empire to go anywhere in the world to do research of importance to their home country's industries. The university proposed two candidates. Our hero, Ernest Rutherford, a physicist, had done his work in the field of electricity and magnetism. The other candidate, James Maclaurin, was a chemist. He had studied a way to extract gold from quartz, a common mineral. Maclaurin's work was deemed more vital to New Zealand's economy, and he was awarded the scholarship. What would become of Rutherford now?

All was not lost. Maclaurin was a married man. One of the conditions for the scholarship was that the winner could not hold a paying job while pursuing his full-time research. Maclaurin was already holding a job that paid thirty pounds a year more than the scholarship offered. (In Rutherford's time the British pound was worth approximately five dollars. The purchasing power of the pound and the dollar was much greater then. Before World War I, a British family could live comfortably in England on 1,000 pounds a year.) Maclaurin was therefore unwilling to give up the job for the scholarship.

Ernest Rutherford would have the chance to study abroad after all.

Ernest's mother was the first to read the telegram bearing the exciting news. She raced out to the vegetable garden to tell her fourth child and second son, Ernest, of his good fortune. According to family lore, Ernest put down his farming tools and said, "That's the last potato I will ever dig."[1] With his 1851 Exhibition Scholarship, Rutherford was able to begin his scientific career as a research student at England's Cavendish Laboratory, half a world away. (The Great Exhibition of 1851 was a world's fair of science and industry held in London. The exhibition was very successful financially. The money it generated not only established several London museums but also led in 1891 to the funding of postgraduate research scholarships.) Over the next twenty years, Rutherford became such a distinguished scientist that in 1919 he was invited to return to the Cavendish as its director.

Perhaps Ernest Rutherford never again cultivated potatoes himself, but he was never embarrassed that his father had earned a living with his hands. Even after Rutherford had been received at Buckingham Palace, he remembered his debt to his parents. In

1931 the British monarch honored him by raising him to the peerage, or nobility. The news arrived at the Rutherford house in the form of a telegram from Ernest himself: "Now Lord Rutherford honour more yours than mine."[2] He often told his mother that everything he had achieved in his life resulted from the sacrifices she and his father had made so that he could be educated.

By 1931 Rutherford had for a decade been a member of the board that decided which students would be granted 1851 Exhibition Scholarships. One year money was tight, and some members of the board suggested that no more scholarships be awarded. Rutherford could be the most jovial of men, but he also had a bad temper. Hearing this suggestion, his face darkened. "If it hadn't been for these scholarships," he sputtered, "I would not have been."[3] His comment made the others realize that the scholarship program must be extended.

There was no reason to suspect that the young New Zealander would grow up to be Lord Rutherford of Nelson, the father of nuclear physics. But by the time Rutherford died in 1937, he had proved his scientific genius by making three major contributions to twentieth-century physics. He solved the mystery of radioactivity, discovered the atomic nucleus, and was the first to deliberately transform one element into another. Two of those contributions came after he won the Nobel Prize! Rutherford also proved to be an outstanding teacher. No fewer than eleven of Rutherford's colleagues and students went on to win Nobel Prizes of their own.

In the last decades of his life, Rutherford focused less on his personal research. In addition to guiding the research of his students, he was busy as a scientific statesman. He was not a political man by nature, but to help other scientists he opposed two fearsome dictatorships, Nazi Germany and the Soviet Union. Under Rutherford's supervision, 20th-century science also moved from "little science" to "big science." Rutherford himself always belonged to what is sometimes called the "sealing wax and string" school of science. This group of scientists devised their own laboratory apparatus out of simple materials and worked alone or with one or two co-workers. But by the end of his life, Rutherford understood that in order to build on the new discoveries he and others had made, big and expensive machines would need to be built.

A young Ernest Rutherford is pictured here in November 1892.

Research teams involving many people would be required. And large sums of money would have to be spent to support the scientific enterprise.

What would have become of Rutherford if he hadn't won the scholarship that took him to England in 1895? We will never know. But we do know that he went on from his humble background to become a great scientist himself, a teacher of many other great scientists, and an influential scientific statesman.

Loss and Luck

NEW ZEALAND WAS STILL A FAIRLY NEW British colony when Ernest Rutherford was born in 1871. For centuries its only inhabitants had been the Maori, a Polynesian people. Although in 1642 the Dutch explorer Abel Tasman became the first European to sight New Zealand, the first Englishman did not set foot there until 1769. As part of his expedition to the South Pacific to observe a transit of Venus across the face of the sun, Captain James Cook of the British navy landed on the North Island, one of New Zealand's two main islands. In the 1790s and early 1800s, hunters, traders, and missionaries began to settle New Zealand. In 1840 the Maori signed a treaty giving Britain control over New Zealand. Twelve years later Britain granted New Zealand a constitution.

Ernest's Rutherford grandparents were among the first British colonists. In 1843 his father's family sailed from Scotland to the South Island, New Zealand's other main island. There Ernest's grandfather helped set up a sawmill. Ernest's father, James, was four years old when they arrived. James would grow up to practice a number of technical trades, including wheelwrighting, saw-milling, bridge construction, flax-farming and processing, and small-scale farming.

Ernest's mother, Martha Thompson Rutherford, was thirteen when she arrived in New Zealand in 1855. Together with her mother and grandmother, who were both widows, Martha made the long sea voyage from Hornchurch, Essex, England, to New Plymouth, on the west coast of New Zealand's North Island. On the North Island, where most of the Maori lived, land disputes with the settlers flared up into a series of wars over the years 1845 to 1872, the year after Ernest's birth. As a result, in 1860, Martha was sent as a war refugee to Nelson, in the northern part of the South Island, along with other women and children from the North Island.

In their new location Martha's mother met and married a farmer from Spring Grove, about thirteen miles south of Nelson. Although today Nelson, with a population of over 53,000 people, is the third largest city in the South Island, then it was a rural pioneering town. First Martha's mother and then Martha herself became the girls' teacher at the 70-pupil school in Spring Grove. When the male head teacher died, Martha became head of the school. In 1866 she married James Rutherford. She retired from her formal teaching career when she became pregnant with the first of their twelve children.

Ernest Rutherford's August 30 birthday made him a winter baby. Since New Zealand lies south of the equator, its seasons are opposite those of the Northern Hemisphere. July and August are usually the coldest months. The Nelson region, however, enjoys mild winters, with temperatures averaging between 36 degrees and 55 degrees Fahrenheit. Throughout most of the year Ernest and his siblings enjoyed collecting birds' nests and other outdoor activities.

Both Martha and James were committed to the belief that knowledge is power: Martha because she had personally benefited from a good education,

A map of New Zealand, where Ernest Rutherford was born, and its surrounding territories.

and James because he had not been so lucky. Martha continued to use her teaching skills to mold her own offspring. Each of the Rutherford children began school knowing the multiplication tables through 12, as well as how to read and spell words of one syllable. In those days before television, VCRs, and computers, the family "entertainment" included spelling bees and quizzes around the fireside at night. On Sunday evenings the family congregated around Martha's piano. Accompanied by James on the violin, the Rutherfords sang songs and hymns.

All the Rutherford children also grew up understanding the importance of hard work and thrift. James Rutherford made a decent living from his series of occupations. But the family was no stranger to hard times, and economic necessity forced them to move on more than one occasion. James often had to work away from home. Wherever they lived, the children were all assigned chores, such as feeding the farm animals, collecting fire wood, and milking the cows. Ernest's older brother, George, was a gifted student. He was never able to realize his dreams of becoming a doctor, however, because he had to help support the large family.

In 1877 the Education Act provided for a free

elementary education for all New Zealand children aged five to fifteen. Ernest began his formal education at the school in Foxhill, on the upper South Island, where the family lived from 1876 to 1883. The school year in New Zealand reflects the flipped seasons, with classes starting in late January and final exams scheduled for December. The long summer vacation occurs during the North American and European winter.

Shortly before his eleventh birthday, while still a student at Foxhill, Ernest was given his first science book. According to its preface, "This book has been written, not so much to give information, as to endeavour to discipline the mind by bringing it into immediate contact with Nature herself, for which purpose a series of simple experiments are described leading up to the chief truths of each science, so that the powers of observation in the pupils may be awakened and strengthened."[1] The book's appendix gave the name of a firm where simple apparatus was available at low cost. For example, one could buy, for a shilling, a "tin pan, with peas" to experiment with the simple effects of gravity or purchase an "iron plate with four strings" to demonstrate the concept of the center of gravity.[2] For the rest of his life,

Rutherford made use of simple apparatus for his pioneering discoveries.

One of the book's experiments explained how to calculate an observer's distance from a cannon using the speed of sound in air and the time lag between the cannon's flash and boom. During a storm young Ernest stunned the family by using this method to determine the approximate distance of each lightning flash. This book also inspired him to make his own miniature cannon with a hat peg, a marble, and blasting powder.

Ernest would later also disassemble and reassemble clocks and make models of the waterwheels that powered his father's mills. As a teenager, after his family moved from the South Island to the scenic Taranaki region in the west of the North Island, Ernest would also make his own cameras and take photographs with them. (New Plymouth, where Ernest's mother had first lived after emigrating to New Zealand, is in the Taranaki region.)

The Rutherford children left Foxhill school in April 1883, during the first semester. James Rutherford had established a flax mill near the head of the Marlborough Sounds, a complex area of waterways on the northern coast of the South Island. To be near him the family moved to Havelock, a small, isolated country town in Marlborough province. The Rutherford family experienced great personal losses in Havelock. A few months after their arrival in May 1883, the last of the Rutherford children, Percy, died of whooping cough at the age of one year and two days. In January 1886, when Ernest was fourteen, his brothers Herbert, aged twelve, and Charles, aged ten, drowned while on a fishing expedition with four other boys who survived. The bodies of the drowned Rutherford boys were never found. Martha Rutherford was sitting at the piano when she heard the news. She never played that instrument again and never regained her formerly upbeat personality. Following the accident, Ernest tried to develop his athletic abilities and learned to swim.

Havelock had another, more positive, impact on Ernest. The schoolmaster there, Jacob Reynolds, was not what we would today consider extremely well educated, but he knew how to turn out academically successful students. (Years later, after Rutherford had been awarded the 1908 Nobel Prize for chemistry, he sent a letter to Reynolds, thanking him "for the way you initiated me into the mysteries of Latin, Algebra and Euclid." Knowing that his former schoolmaster was out of a job, Rutherford enclosed a check for 20 pounds out of the 7,680-pound award money.)[3]

When Ernest turned fifteen in August 1886, he would no longer be entitled to a free education. If he wanted to go to secondary school he would have to win an Education Board scholarship to the nearest secondary school, Nelson College. (In some countries the word "college" sometimes refers to a private secondary school and sometimes to a unit of a university. Thus Rutherford was first a high school student at Nelson College and then a university student at Canterbury College of the University of New Zealand.) Only one such scholarship was available for all the children throughout Marlborough province. Reynolds tutored Ernest and several other students to help them prepare for the December 1885 scholarship test. Although Ernest came in second of 62 candidates, he did not win the single scholarship.

Because he did not win the scholarship, Ernest Rutherford almost became a civil servant instead of a physicist. In those days a New Zealander was considered old enough to begin a career in the civil service at fifteen. Thus, in late October 1886, two months after he turned fifteen, Ernest took the two-day Junior Civil Service Exam. He was the only candidate from Havelock to do so. The subjects covered included English, arithmetic, history, and geography. He came in 15th of the 202 New Zealanders who took that exam, but a full year passed before he was offered a civil service position.

The delay proved lucky, however. Nelson College had a rule that all applicants for the Education Board scholarship had to be under age fifteen—except for those students applying from rural Marlborough province, whose educational progress might be expected to be on the slow side. Therefore, Ernest was eligible to take the scholarship exam a second time. When he took the 1886 exam, he was, at the age of fifteen years and three months, the second oldest candidate for the Education Board scholarship to Nelson College. Sixteen students from the province were competing for the single scholarship. Understanding how crucial the outcome of this exam was, Ernest got up at 5:00 A.M. each day to study. His efforts paid off: This time Ernest came in first among all the applicants from

Marlborough province. The scholarship he won would cover two years of board and fees.

Nelson College had been established in 1856, making it New Zealand's oldest state secondary school. The college still exists, offering academic classes, along with sports and cultural activities for boys. When Ernest began the academic year in February 1887, there were only 80 students at Nelson College, ranging in age from ten to twenty-one. Of those only 25 were boarding students who lived in the school's dormitories. The boarders had a strict schedule that took them from wake-up at 6:30 A.M. through "candles out" before 10:00 P.M. They were not allowed to go into the dorm area during the school day and needed permission to leave the school grounds.

Nelson College's 80 students were taught by only four teachers, or "masters." In terms of Ernest's future career, his most important master was William Still Littlejohn. Littlejohn had a master's degree from Aberdeen University in Scotland in classics—the languages and literature of ancient Greece and Rome. Since another master taught those subjects at Nelson, it was Littlejohn who gave Ernest a solid foundation in mathematics and introduced him to physics and chemistry. Many years later, when Littlejohn died at the age of seventy-four, his former pupil was already Lord Rutherford of Nelson. The now distinguished alumnus of Nelson College looked back gratefully on Littlejohn as "a man of broad humanity and tolerance who laboured unceasingly by precept and example to develop the intelligence and character of the boys under his charge."[4] After Rutherford's death in 1937, a classmate from Nelson sent a letter to *The Times* of London, recalling Ernest's habit in those days "of strolling about with Mr. W. S. Littlejohn on the half-holiday, up and down little frequented streets near the College, Littlejohn drawing diagrams in the dust of Hampden Street and discussing them with Rutherford."[5]

In later years Ernest's schoolmates would recall how completely absorbed he would become in trying to solve a math problem. More than one rascal would bop the studious Ernest on the head, knowing he would be able to run off without provoking a bop in return. As focused as he was while working out math problems, however, Ernest was a fine all-around scholar. While at Nelson he showed no special inclination toward a career in science. The headmaster would later remember Ernest as having "displayed some capacity for mathematics and physics but not to an abnormal degree. He was a keen footballer and a popular boy."[6] In any case, Nelson College did not really have a proper science laboratory until 1890, the year after Ernest left. Nonetheless, before leaving Nelson for good at the end of 1889, Ernest became the owner of a university-level book describing experiments and equipment in the field of sound and light.

Ernest's general academic success turned out to be a crucial factor in enabling him to go to university. At the end of his first year at Nelson, his work in classics earned him a scholarship worth 20 pounds for one year. He also won a history scholarship, which provided another 20 pounds a year for three years. At the end of his remaining years at Nelson, he won additional prizes worth considerable amounts of money in subjects including English literature, French, and math.

When Ernest returned to Nelson for his second year in early 1888, he hoped to win a scholarship to the University of New Zealand for the academic year beginning in 1889. His scholarship to Nelson, after all, was good for only two years. Mr. Littlejohn coached Ernest in the evenings to help him prepare for the university entrance exams as well as for the scholarship exams. Only 10 of these scholarships were available for all of New Zealand. In December 1888 Ernest took both sets of exams. When the results were published, he learned that he had qualified for admission to university, but he had not won a scholarship.

Although Ernest's scholarship to Nelson would not cover his fees for a third year there, his school prize money would. As a result, Ernest was able to return to Nelson in 1889. He returned to the highest leadership role a student can have in the British school system—he was "head boy." The head boy is sometimes called "Dux"—the Latin word for leader or chief—which led to Ernest's nickname, "Quacks."

Before taking the scholarship exams for the second time, Ernest decided he had better have alternative plans in case he failed again. He applied for a position teaching physical science at a high school in New Plymouth, where his mother had lived as a teenager and near where his parents currently lived. A week before he learned the outcome of the scholarship exam, Ernest found out that the teaching job had gone to a university student with some teaching experience. By the end of the week, however, he learned that, having earned the fourth-highest marks on the scholarship exam, he had won a scholarship to the University of New Zealand.

Once again we can ask "What if?" about Ernest Rutherford. What would have become of him if he had not won scholarships to Nelson College and the University of New Zealand, each on the second try? Would he have become, as Rutherford once confided to a friend, "a farmer and never realized his special gifts"?[7] The answer to that question must remain unknown. But we do know that in the next stage of his life, at Canterbury College, young Ernest Rutherford not only discovered a passion for research but also found the love of his life.

Research and Romance

CANTERBURY COLLEGE WAS ONLY SIXTEEN years old when eighteen-year-old Ernest arrived in Christchurch in March 1890, the beginning of the school year. It was the second oldest of the then three branches of the University of New Zealand. Ernest was among 150 full-time students enrolled that year. The college employed only a handful of professors to teach all of them and the 150 part-time students. Ernest signed up for the three-year program leading to the bachelor of arts, or B.A., degree. In addition to the required courses in Latin and math, over the years he chose to study applied math, English, French, and physics.

Ernest hit his stride as a student at the beginning

of his college career and never slackened. At the end of each of his first three years in Christchurch, he was awarded a math prize worth 20 pounds, sometimes sharing it with a classmate. It took him some time, however, to develop the outgoing, confident personality for which he was famous later in life. He joined the college debating society shortly after arriving, for example, but participated only as a spectator for his first two years. One of his classmates his first year remembered him as "very modest, friendly but rather shy and rather vague—a man who had not yet found himself and was not then conscious of his extraordinary powers."[1]

Ernest seems to have entered more fully into campus social life in his final B.A. year. He was elected treasurer of the college debating society and argued in support of the motion that "the influence of the modern newspaper press is excessive and dangerous."[2] In 1893 he was elected to the committee of the College Lawn Tennis Club and assistant secretary of the Football Club. He also played forward in the football club's first team.

Ernest spent the long school vacations in his family's isolated farm house in Pungarehu, in the Taranaki region of the North Island. His mother sometimes asked Ernest to occupy his three youngest sisters by teaching them some material. He agreed to do so, on condition that his mother assemble the girls. He used novel ways to keep them focused on his lesson. For example, he kept the girls from fidgeting by tying each one's braids to those of her sister.

Beginning in his second year at Canterbury College, Ernest took part in the newly formed Science Society. As the highlight of its first season, the society held an open night one Saturday that was attended by about 800 people. Members of the society, including Ernest, displayed scientific apparatus. The next day he wrote home describing his role in the event: "I was boss of what they called the 'darkroom' in which I had to exhibit a good deal of apparatus. . . . They consisted of spectroscopes to show the spectra of solar light, light of a gas flame, candle, etc. . . . I explained my apparatus for about 3 hours before a continually changing audience, when I went and had a look round the show myself."[3] To recover from the successful event, he spent the next day "loafing all day long reading and doing nothing." Throughout his life he continued to enjoy reading books on a wide variety of subjects.

It was not until the second term of his second

year at Canterbury College that Ernest began a course in experimental physics. The thirty-one students in this course learned to use thermometers and other instruments to study heat, spectroscopes and other tools to study light and sound, and batteries and other apparatus to study electricity and magnetism. The professor for this course was Alexander Bickerton. Bickerton—or "Bicky," as the students called him—was a bit of an eccentric. Neither Bickerton nor the students found the lab facilities adequate. The "Tin Shed" that served as the lab both for physics and chemistry was a galvanized iron building about sixty feet long. All of the apparatus had to be assembled and disassembled before each session, and nothing could be left there.

A little more room was found for physics experiments in the "Tin Shed" for the following academic year, 1892. That year Ernest took a course in honors physics. He passed his B.A. at the end of 1892 with first-class honors in physics.

His academic career at Christchurch, however, was not yet over. At the end of 1892, Ernest once again took exams for a scholarship. He hoped to do well enough to get funding for an additional year's work. The future physicist won the scholarship based on his exams in math and mathematical physics, not in physics and physical science. He was awarded a master's degree (M.A.) at the end of 1893 with double first-class honors in both fields. That year Ernest was the only student to obtain first-class honors in either math or physics. Not since 1887 had a science student succeeded in achieving a double honors degree.

The academic year 1893 was a crucial one in Ernest's life. He was transformed into a research scientist. Having to struggle to make the best of inadequate lab conditions was not necessarily a bad thing. He later recalled, "I learnt more of research methods in those first investigations under somewhat difficult conditions than in any work I have done since."[4] Ernest decided to do original research in the field of electricity and magnetism. He had some help from the lab assistant in designing and setting up his equipment, but he did the research entirely on his own.

Professor Bickerton recognized Ernest's potential right away. He later wrote, "From the first he exhibited an unusual aptitude for experimental science and in research work showed originality and capacity of a high order."[5] Bickerton's main contribution to Ernest's project was helping him find space in which to carry it out. Ernest's experiments involved some measurements with an instrument that was very sensitive to vibration. Since there was no physics lab, Ernest tried to work both in the Tin Shed and in a large multi-purpose room. The instrument's readings would be disturbed every time someone entered the room. Bickerton got permission for Ernest to use a den where he could work undisturbed. Rutherford later described the den as a "miserable, cold, draughty, concrete-floored cellar" where the students "were accustomed to hang up their caps and gowns," the clothes they were required to wear on the college grounds.[6] In these less than ideal surroundings, however, he managed to develop a timing device that could switch circuits in less than one-hundred-thousandth of a second.

After finishing his 1893 end-of-year exams, Ernest took out a book that had recently arrived at the Canterbury College library. It was a collection of mathematical and physical papers by Lord Kelvin. Lord Kelvin (1824–1907) was one of the major physicists and mathematicians of the day. His contributions in several fields helped shape the scientific thought of his era. One of the articles in Kelvin's book, about the passage of a temporary current of electricity through an iron bar, gave Ernest some ideas about a new use for his equipment. Little did he know that within the next decade he would not only meet the great Lord Kelvin as an equal but would also have the chance to prove him wrong on a scientific point.

As Christmas 1893 drew near, Ernest traveled home for the summer vacation by steamship. He did not yet know how he had done on his exams for the master's degree. He also did not know what he would be doing next. Before leaving Christchurch he had sent in an application to the Boys' High School that was run by the Board of Governors of Canterbury College. The school was looking for an assistant master to begin work in February 1894 "to teach the usual secondary subjects, including French and Elementary Science."[7] There were fifty-seven other applicants for the position. Ernest, who had less experience than many of them, was not hired.

Ernest returned to Canterbury College for the academic year 1894 even though he had no financial aid. He had decided to apply for a research scholarship overseas. He had to be an enrolled student in order to do so. To pay his tuition and living expenses, he tutored other students. His father and older brother, George, may have helped him out financially.

Ernest had set his sights on the 1851 Exhibition Scholarship. It was worth 150 pounds per year for two years. Outstanding research students from Great Britain, Ireland, Canada, Australia, and New Zealand attempted to demonstrate that their original work could advance the industry of their native land. The winners could use the scholarship anywhere in the world. The University of New Zealand arranged with the board of commissioners of the scholarship to evaluate candidates' research at the end of November 1894. The university would then choose a single winner.

Ernest spent the year performing research on the magnetization of iron. He wanted to determine whether iron was really as strongly magnetic as supposed. Once again it was important to find a suitable place to do his work. Ernest explained in a letter to the administration that "the vibration of a wooden building is fatal to the accuracy of observations."[8] An appropriate basement room was found.

At the end of 1894 Ernest submitted two research reports. The first described the research he had performed in 1893. The second described his 1894 research. It reviewed previous groundbreaking work in the field of electricity, including the contributions of Heinrich Hertz (1857–1894) and J. J. Thomson (1856–1940). Less than a decade before, Heinrich Hertz in Germany had detected the radio waves that had been predicted by James Clerk Maxwell's (1831–1879) theory of electromagnetism. Maxwell, who ranks with Newton and Einstein as one of the greatest physicists of all time, had found a set of equations that revealed that electricity and magnetism were linked and were different aspects of a single force known as the electromagnetic force. J. J. Thomson, Maxwell's successor as director of the world-famous Cavendish Laboratory in Cambridge, England, was currently doing pioneering electrical work there.

At that early stage in the study of Maxwell's linked electricity and magnetism, it was known that rapidly changing electric currents could cause a magnetic field to form. We still generate and modify electricity by using "transformers," which contain iron wrapped with wires that carry a changing electric current. How deeply the iron was magnetized by a changing electric current seemed to depend on how fast the current changed. According to Hertz, Thomson, and other top physicists of the day, if the electric current changed too fast, no magnetic field would form in the iron.

In his second research report Ernest explained how his original research had proved "that iron still keeps its magnetic properties" at very high frequencies.[9] In his primitive basement laboratory he had devised experiments that showed that Hertz, Thomson, and the others were wrong: A magnetic field formed in iron even when the current oscillated very rapidly, half a billion times per second. His report thus challenged the conclusions of some of the greatest physicists of the day. Ernest would shortly realize that his discoveries about electricity and magnetism would enable him to invent a device for detecting wireless signals, which we now call radio waves.

While writing up his research reports, Ernest had an unexpected opportunity to teach at Boys' High School. The math teacher had fallen ill. As his substitute, Ernest earned about four pounds a week. One of the boys he taught later remembered, "He

J. J. Thomson and Ernest Rutherford (left to right) share a conversation in June 1934.

was entirely hopeless as a schoolmaster. Disorder prevailed in his classes." It didn't take the students long to figure out that their twenty-three-year-old substitute teacher was "a genial person whose interests were nothing to do with the keeping in order of small boys."[10]

The end of 1894 was very busy for Ernest, but it was filled with uncertainty about the future. He submitted his research reports, tutored students, coached his schoolboys for their math finals, and took his own exams for the B.Sc. Then he went home to his family for Christmas to await the decision on the 1851 Exhibition Scholarship. Ernest must have been dejected when he was informed that the other University of New Zealand applicant had been selected.

By late April 1895 an article in a local newspaper announced that Ernest Rutherford had been selected "by the University Senate for the Science Research Scholarship granted by the Commissioners of the 1851 Exhibition" for his "long and valuable research in Electricity and Magnetism."[11] The matter was not fully settled, however, until July 9. That was the day Ernest's mother received the telegram indicating that her son would never need to dig another potato. He had won the approval of the board of commissioners of the 1851 Exhibition Scholarship, thus becoming the first New Zealand student to be awarded that scholarship in physics.

Less than a month later, on August 1, 1895, Ernest Rutherford set sail for England. He had to borrow money to pay for his passage. From the ship he began a correspondence with the girl he left behind, for in Christchurch he had matured not only as a scientist but also as a man. When he had begun as a B.A. student, he had shared rooms off campus with two fellow students. Perhaps as early as 1891, however, he began to board with a widow, Mrs. Mary Newton. Mrs. Newton's husband had died in 1888 at thirty-five, leaving her alone with four young children. The oldest was a girl, Mary Georgina, called "May." May Newton was about five years younger than Ernest.

In May 1893 Ernest's older brother, George, became the first of the family to meet the Newtons. While in Christchurch en route to Australia on behalf of the Rutherford family flax business, George wrote in his diary that Mrs. Newton "says she looks upon Ern as one of her family. She is very proud of his success."[12] By Christmas 1894 it seemed certain that the Rutherfords and the Newtons would in fact become one family. Ernest arranged to have May Newton, now eighteen, spend the month of February 1895 with the Rutherford family in Pungarehu. Ernest's sisters were not impressed with May during that visit—they thought she was spoiled. She and Ernest's brothers got along so well, however, that May said in jest to James Rutherford, "Well, Mr. Rutherford, if I cannot have your Ern I will have one of your other sons."[13] By the time Ernest left for England, the couple was unofficially engaged. Their families agreed that the marriage would not take place until he could afford to support a wife. Who could predict how long that would take?

May Newton was disappointed in the letters Ernest wrote from the ship carrying him far from home. He responded that she would "have to get accustomed" to his failure to express gushy sentiments: "I don't naturally take to being very loving on paper."[14] The letters he continued to write her over the years—as her boyfriend, then fiancé, then husband—may have dissatisfied May, but they provide a great deal of information about the career of the man who was soon to become the major physicist of his generation.

From Radio to Radioactivity

ERNEST RUTHERFORD ARRIVED IN ENGLAND on September 20, 1895. Exactly three weeks earlier he had turned twenty-four on shipboard. He spent the next week in London. In a letter dated September 24, J. J. Thomson welcomed him "to work at the Cavendish Laboratory," promising him "all the assistance I can." J.J. (as everyone called him) invited Rutherford "to come to Cambridge for a few hours" so that he could learn more about Rutherford's "requirements and intentions."[1]

Rutherford took the train to Cambridge, where the meeting went well. A few days later he wrote a letter to May summarizing his first impressions: "I went to the Lab and saw Thomson and had a good long talk with him. He is very pleasant in conversation and is not fossilized at all. . . . We discussed matters in general and research work, and he seemed pleased with what I was going to do." He reported also that J.J. had invited him home for lunch. There he met "Mrs. J.J.," who was very welcoming, as well as the Thomsons' toddler— "the best little kid I have seen for looks and size."[2]

No one at the Thomson home that day could know that three of those present were future winners of the Nobel Prize. The toddler grew up to be physicist Sir George Paget Thomson (1892–1975). In 1937, the year Rutherford died, G. P. Thomson shared the Nobel Prize for physics for his work on electrons (subatomic particles with a negative electric charge). J.J.'s studies of the effects of electricity on gases had led to the discovery of the electron in February 1897. For these studies J.J. received the Nobel Prize for physics in 1906. (Rutherford would receive the Nobel Prize for chemistry in 1908.)

Rutherford became the first postgraduate research student at the University of Cambridge whose earlier work had been done at another university. Several others arrived shortly after he did.

These men ended up socializing together. J.J. did whatever he could to make these new research students fit in. Some of the "demonstrators," or lab instructors, however, were resentful of the newcomers and did their best to make them feel unwelcome.

By the time Rutherford arrived in Cambridge, he had with him a device of his own invention that could detect wireless signals. He had made every part of it himself, including the electric batteries. J.J. later wrote in his autobiography, "Rutherford began his work at the Laboratory by working at wireless telegraphy, using a detector which he had invented before leaving New Zealand. . . . He held, not long after he had been at work in the Laboratory, the record for long-distance telegraphy, as he had succeeded in sending messages from the Laboratory to his rooms about three-quarters of a mile away."[3]

Most people would identify Italian inventor Guglielmo Marconi as the first to send and detect radio communication signals through the air. Rutherford, however, using his own detector, did pioneering work in that field. According to the 1902 *Encyclopaedia Britannica*, "A very efficient detector, indeed by far the simplest and best for metrical work, is that invented by Rutherford. . . . Rutherford in 1895 got indications when the vibrator was three-quarters of a mile away and the waves had to traverse a *thickly populated part* of Cambridge."[4] In 1910 Rutherford wrote in a history of the Cavendish Laboratory that his early experiments there "were made before Marconi began his well-known investigations on signalling by electrical waves."[5]

News of Rutherford and his detector spread through the university and beyond. The director of the Cambridge University Observatory, Sir Robert Ball, immediately saw the application of Rutherford's work to navigation. If a lighthouse could transmit wireless signals to receivers onboard ships, accidents in fog could be avoided. Anxious to get married as soon as possible, Rutherford began to imagine that income stemming from his radio research might enable him to do so. He wrote May, "The reason I am so keen on the subject [of radio detection] is because of its practical importance. . . . If my next week's experiments come out as well as I anticipate, I see a chance of making cash rapidly in the future."[6] On Rutherford's behalf, J.J. inquired about the commercial value of a system of wireless communication. He was given the incorrect prediction that such a scheme—radio—was unlikely to be worth much! In order to help Rutherford earn enough money to marry, J.J. began to find students for him to tutor, exams for him to administer, and books for him to review.

Even if the work would not make his talented research student from New Zealand a rich man, J.J. realized that it was worth presenting to the Royal Society, the oldest and most prestigious scientific society in Great Britain. On June 18, 1896, Rutherford had the honor of explaining the principles of his radio-wave detector to the fellows of the Royal Society. Rutherford also wrote a paper, "A Magnetic Detector of Electrical Waves and Some of Its Applications," which was accepted for publication in the Royal Society's journal, *Philosophical Transactions*. ("Natural philosophy" is an old-fashioned name for physics.) J.J. began to tell people that Rutherford's contributions in and of themselves justified the university's having opened its doors to research students from other institutions.

By then, however, J.J. had other research plans for his gifted student. In November 1895, German physicist Wilhelm Roentgen (1845–1923) discovered a new kind of ray. He called it the X-ray, with X standing for "unknown." Roentgen took photographs that showed how X-rays could travel through solid substances. On February 27, 1896, J.J. wrote in the British science journal *Nature*, "The discovery by Professor Roentgen of the rays which bear his name has aroused an interest unparalleled in the history of physical science . . . experiments seem to show that these rays exert a powerful disintegrating effect on the molecules of substances through which they pass, and suggest that their use may throw light on some questions of molecular structure."[7]

The unidentified new ray immediately stimulated interest in laboratories around the world. The Cavendish was no exception. In a letter to May in late January 1896, Rutherford reported that J.J. had "been very busy lately over the new method of photography discovered by Professor Roentgen. . . . The professor of course is trying to find out the real cause and nature of the waves, and the great object is to find the theory of the matter before anyone else, for nearly every Professor in Europe is now on the warpath."[8]

In mid-April 1896, J.J. enlisted Rutherford to collaborate with him in studying the electrical effect of X-rays on gases. Rutherford wrote back to New Zealand, "I am a little full up of my old subject and am glad of a change. I expect it will be a good thing for me to work with the Professor for a time. I have done one research to show I can work by myself."[9] He continued his wireless work on his own time, however.

By autumn 1896 professor and student had completed their joint work. At a meeting of the British Association for the Advancement of Science in September, J.J. delivered a paper on their findings. He pointed out that X-rays cause gases to change from electrical insulators, through which electrical current does not pass easily, to electrical conductors, through which it does pass easily. The researchers interpreted their results correctly as proving that X-rays were electromagnetic waves, similar to light. Their work was published in the important physics journal *Philosophical Magazine*.

J.J. had other things on his mind besides X-rays. In February 1897 he performed on his own the experiment that showed the existence of electrons. This discovery upset the long-held belief that the smallest particle of matter was the atom, and that the atom itself could not be subdivided or changed.

Just as the professor had moved on to work of his

own, so had his research student. First Rutherford studied the electrical effects of ultraviolet light. He concluded they were similar to those of X-rays. Next he turned his attention to the electrical effects of another new type of ray. In early 1896, a few months after Roentgen discovered X-rays, French physicist Henri Becquerel accidentally discovered that a sample of uranium ore emitted rays that could fog a photographic plate even without exposure to light. Few scientists paid much attention to these "Becquerel rays" or "uranium rays," which were not as spectacular as X-rays.

In 1897 Marie Curie in Paris and Rutherford in Cambridge independently set out to understand the nature of these rays. Within a year, Marie Curie, joined in her investigation by her husband, Pierre, had found two new elements that emitted Becquerel rays. The Curies named the newly discovered elements polonium and radium. Rutherford's preliminary work also uncovered two previously unidentified phenomena, although they were not new elements. As J.J. later described in his autobiography, "Rutherford . . . investigated the radiation from uranium very thoroughly. He found that the radiation was of two types, one type, which he called the alpha type, being absorbed after passing through a few millimeters of air, while the other, the beta type, could get through more than twenty times this distance."[10] (Later, after leaving the Cavendish, Rutherford also studied the electrical effects of the rays from thorium compounds. In doing so, he detected an even more penetrating kind of ray, which was later named the gamma ray by another scientist. *Alpha, beta,* and *gamma* are the first three letters in the Greek alphabet.)

Over the course of 1897–1898 Rutherford continued his work at the Cavendish on the rays emitted by uranium. Since his two-year 1851 Exhibition Scholarship of 150 pounds would run out in summer 1897, at J.J.'s recommendation, Rutherford applied for an extension to a third year. In J.J.'s letter of support to the board of commissioners, he wrote that Rutherford "is quite in the first rank of physicists. . . . If it is not contrary to the rules to renew his Scholarship, I am sure such a proceeding would tend greatly to the advancement of Physical Science."[11] In addition, Rutherford won another scholarship that provided 250 pounds for two years.

During a long visit to England in spring 1897, May Newton was able to attend the ceremony at which Ernest was awarded his Cambridge B.A. for his research. Her visit, however, only heightened his eagerness to get married. Even though he would only turn twenty-seven that August, he hoped to be appointed professor somewhere. A professor's stable position and salary could make an early marriage possible.

McGill University in Montreal, Canada, advertised an opening in the physics department for the academic year beginning in autumn 1898. The senior professor of physics and the principal of McGill came to Cambridge to interview Rutherford. J.J. wrote him a glowing letter of recommendation: "I have never had a student with more enthusiasm or ability for original research than Mr. Rutherford and I am sure that if elected he would establish a distinguished school of Physics at Montreal. I should consider any Institution fortunate that secured the services of Mr. Rutherford as a Professor of Physics."[12]

On August 3, 1898, Rutherford was able to write to May Newton: "Rejoice with me, my dear girl, for matrimony is looming in the distance. I got word on Monday . . . to say I was appointed to Montreal."[13] He had already calculated, however, that it would

The physics building at McGill University, named for Ernest Rutherford.
Rutherford taught at the Canadian school from 1898 to 1907.

make financial sense to put off the marriage for another year "to get enough cash to do it in style."[14]

May was a little disappointed that her fiancé preferred the McGill appointment to a possible position at the branch of the University of New Zealand in Wellington. If Ernest were appointed to a professorship there, they would be able to marry immediately. The salary offered at Wellington was 200 pounds a year more than at McGill, and they would be close to their families. He explained that "my chances of advancement are much better in McGill, than if I got out to New Zealand." Among other considerations, the physics facilities at McGill—provided by the generosity of a tobacco millionaire—were among the best in the world. "There is also a certain amount of satisfaction in having a swell lab under one's control, and probably in New Zealand my chances of research work would be very small."[15]

Five weeks after learning of his appointment, Rutherford set off by ship for the next stage of his career. When he had left New Zealand three years earlier, he had needed to borrow the money for the fare. This time, thanks to the generosity of McGill, he could afford to make the crossing in a first-class cabin. He confided in May some of his worries about living up to expectations: "I am expected to do a lot of original work and to form a research school in order to knock the shine out of the Yankees!"[16] Knowing that some of his future colleagues at McGill were his own age, he wrote, "It sounds rather comic to myself to have to supervise the research of other men, but I hope I will get along all right."[17]

Over the course of the next nine years, Ernest Rutherford got along much better than all right. Led by him, researchers assembled at McGill did detective work that led to a new understanding of matter and energy. In 1898 Marie Curie coined the word *radioactivity* to describe the behavior of elements whose compounds spontaneously emit Becquerel rays. Ernest Rutherford would become the major figure in solving what remained for the moment the mystery of radioactivity. He would eventually oversee its development into nuclear physics.

The Mysteries of Radioactivity

JUST BEFORE RUTHERFORD SET SAIL FOR Canada, he ordered some uranium and thorium salts—bits of solid matter that contained enough of those elements to make them experimentally useful. Although he did not know it at the time, his work with these raw materials would shortly lead to a revolution in scientific thought. After arriving in Montreal and settling in, Rutherford plunged into the responsibilities of his new job. He was based in McGill's Macdonald Physics Building, or MPB. The MPB was still a fairly new facility. At the time of its opening in 1893, it was the most expensive physics lab in the world. Sir William Macdonald had made his millions by selling tobacco to the Union army during the American Civil War. He personally considered smoking a filthy habit and lived a very simple life, though he lavished money on McGill University.

Luckily for Rutherford, the new position did not require him to do too much teaching. He was already quite an effective public speaker, able to interest an audience in a topic about which he was passionate. Teaching elementary material to barely willing young students, however, was not among his strengths, as he had already learned at the Christchurch Boys' School.

Rutherford threw himself into his research. He immediately began noticing unexpected things about his radioactive samples. For example, he detected what he called an "emanation" given off by thorium. The properties of the emanation were not the same as those of thorium itself. The emanation, he began to suspect, must be a radioactive gas not of thorium but of a different radioactive substance! He noticed that the radioactivity of the emanation gradually decreased. Always a stickler for exact measurements, he noted that in one minute, the sample of radioactive material was reduced by half. After two minutes, only a quarter of the original value remained. After three minutes, only an eighth of the original volume remained. It was as if he was watching the water in a bathtub drain out in a very regular fashion, with half of the remaining water in the tub draining out as each minute ticked by.

Without hesitation, Rutherford brought in other scientists at McGill whose areas of expertise he sensed would help move his intriguing work along. He felt a great deal of pressure to make progress. As he wrote his mother in early 1902, "I have to keep going as there are always people on my track. I have to publish my present work as rapidly as possible in order to keep in the race. The best sprinters in this road of investigation are Becquerel and the Curies in Paris who have done a great deal of very important work in the subject of radioactive bodies during the last few years."[1]

Rutherford's most important partnership at McGill, and one of the most fruitful in the history of science, was with chemist Frederick Soddy (1877–1956). The collaboration began in October 1901 and ended with Soddy's departure for England in early 1903. Within that brief time, Rutherford and Soddy figured out the basic mystery of radioactivity. Looking back on their work years later, Soddy recalled: "By the time our cooperation ended, radioactivity, which had already become a considerable jigsaw puzzle, had been put together, and my chief impression of those days remains of an intense mental exaltation as the pieces came together and they were fitted by the single theory of atomic disintegration into a convincing whole."[2]

Rutherford and Soddy's revolutionary theory explained the mysterious phenomena they and other scientists were discovering about radioactivity. The research led them to conclude that radioactive elements actually transform themselves into other elements. They spontaneously break apart, or decay, into other elements. As they do so, they radiate tiny particles and energetic waves. (The alpha and beta radiation Rutherford had named at the Cavendish turned out to be particles. The gamma radiation named by another scientist turned out to be electromagnetic waves, like light or radio waves, but with much more energy.) When a radioactive material gives off alpha or beta particles, it changes into an atom of another element.

An important piece of Rutherford and Soddy's theory was the idea of half-life. Radioactive decay occurs at different rates in different elements or different forms of the same element. A succession of decays take place until what is left at the end is a stable, or nonradioactive, element. Uranium, for example, goes through a succession of decays until it ends up as a form of lead that is not radioactive. We measure the rate of decay by the half-life, the length of time it takes for half the atoms in a sample to decay. The half-life of the most common form of uranium, for example, is 4.5 billion years. Over that immense time (about the age of the Earth), half the atoms in a sample will spontaneously transform themselves into one nonradioactive form of lead. A much less common form of uranium has a half-life of over 700 million years. A third, very rare, form of uranium has a half-life of about 250,000 years.

Rutherford and Soddy called the original radioactive atom that undergoes decay the parent, and the series of atoms into which it is transformed the daughters. The two elements Marie Curie discovered, polonium and radium, are both radioactive decay products, or daughters, of uranium.

By the time that Rutherford and Soddy began their historic collaboration, Rutherford had become a parent with a daughter of his own. In April 1900 he finally returned to New Zealand to marry May Newton. Their small wedding took place on June 28. When he and May returned to Montreal in the autumn, she was already pregnant. A daughter, whom they named Eileen, was born at the end of March 1901. Rutherford wrote his mother, "The baby is of course a marvel of intelligence and we think there never was such a fine baby before."[3] Although Rutherford adored children, Eileen was an only child.

On his trip back to New Zealand to marry May, Rutherford also applied for a doctorate of science (D.Sc.) from the University of New Zealand. He submitted all his published papers. As of February 1901, he could officially be called "Dr. Rutherford."

As satisfied as Rutherford was with the lab facilities and light teaching duties at McGill, he nonetheless felt cut off from the center of scientific life in England. In those days, before e-mail and faxes, it took a long time to communicate scientific results. In February 1900, a few months before they married, Rutherford wrote May, "I don't think you will mind Canada for a few years for, between you and me, I don't regard myself as finally settled here, but hope to get over to England some day."[4] As early as March 1901, Rutherford let J. J. Thomson know that he would be happy to return to England if the right position could be found. "After the years in the Cavendish I feel myself rather out of things scientific, and greatly miss the opportunities of meeting men interested in physics. Outside the small circle of the laboratory it is seldom I meet anyone to hear what is being done elsewhere."[5]

In 1903 a full version of the revolutionary Rutherford-Soddy theory of radioactive decay was published. In 1904 Rutherford published his first book, under the simple title *Radioactivity*. Dedicated to J. J. Thomson, the book states clearly that radioactivity is a property of the atom, and that the atom is a storehouse of energy: "an enormous store of latent energy is resident in the radioactive atoms themselves." Scientists had not previously observed the energy inside the atom because they had no way "of breaking up into simpler forms the atoms of the elements by the action of the chemical or physical forces at our command."[6] Rutherford's work helped shatter the formerly held belief that the atom was like a tiny billiard ball that could not be subdivided. It did not, however, suggest any way of splitting the atom to release the enormous energy inside it.

Rutherford began to get offers from prestigious universities in the United States, including Columbia and Yale. Neither interested him. Before the scientific and technological advances made during World War II, science facilities at American universities lagged behind those in England and Europe. Longing to find the right job that would bring him back to England, he was happy in 1903 to learn he had been elected a Fellow of the Royal Society (FRS), a very prestigious honor.

The following year found him in England not for a new position but for two important lectures. The more prestigious of the two was the Royal Society's Bakerian Lecture. Those annual lectures dated back to 1775, when they were funded by a bequest from a former FRS, Henry Baker. In his Bakerian Lecture Rutherford presented the theory of radioactivity. Later that year the Royal Society honored him again. He received the Rumford Medal of the Royal Society, which is awarded every second year "to the author of the most important discovery or useful improvement which shall be made . . . during the preceding two years . . . , the preference always being given to such discoveries as . . . tend most to promote the good of mankind."[7]

Rutherford's second important lecture on his spring 1904 trip to England was given to the

Royal Institution. Since 1799 the goal of the Royal Institution had been "diffusing science for the common purposes of life."[8] At his lecture Rutherford presented a new and important theory. This theory, about the age of the earth, challenged the opinion of Lord Kelvin, the grand old man of British physics. Since Lord Kelvin was in the audience, Rutherford found himself in a ticklish situation.

Rutherford was the first to see that the radioactive theory of decay provided a clue to the age of the earth. He understood that the decaying elements inside rocks function like clocks, ticking off the years since the rocks formed. Radioactive dating is based on the idea that radioactive elements like uranium have been steadily decaying since the formation of the earth. For example, it should be possible to measure the age of the rocks containing uranium ores by comparing the amount of the parent radioactive element with the final daughter, a stable form of lead. The stable form of lead is never present when the rocks form. So if a rock contains equal amounts of uranium, with a half-life of 4.5 billion years, and lead, the rock sample must be one half-life, or 4.5 billion years, old.

Rutherford also believed that the earth's interior was hot because of the energy given off during the radioactive decay of uranium into radium, one of its daughters. Long before the discovery of radioactivity, Lord Kelvin had done measurements of the rate at which energy escaped from the earth as heat. These measurements led Lord Kelvin to conclude that the earth was only between 20 and 40 million years old. This age seemed much too young to geologists, who thought that rocks were at least 100 million years old. In his lecture at the Royal Institution, Rutherford explained why the geologists were right and Lord Kelvin was wrong. A comparison of the earth's present temperature with the amount of heat provided by the radioactive decay of radioactive elements since its formation showed that the earth must be at least several hundreds of millions years old. (Since Rutherford's time more accurate methods of radioactive dating have shown that the age of the earth and the rest of the solar system is about 4.55 billion years.)

After the Royal Institution lecture, Rutherford enjoyed entertaining people by describing the event in this way: "I came into the room, which was half dark, and presently spotted Lord Kelvin in the audience and realised that I was in for trouble at the last part of my speech dealing with the age of the earth, where my views conflicted with his. To my relief, Kelvin fell fast asleep, but as I came to the important point, I saw the old bird sit up, open an eye and cock a baleful glance at me! Then a sudden inspiration came, and I said Lord Kelvin had limited the age of the earth, *provided no new source was discovered*. That prophetic utterance refers to what we are now considering tonight, radium! Behold! the old boy beamed upon me."[9]

As Rutherford's reputation around the world grew, postgraduate researchers from other countries sought out the opportunity to work with him at McGill, just as he had sought out the opportunity of working with J. J. Thomson at the Cavendish. The most famous of the foreign researchers who came to work with Rutherford at McGill was Otto Hahn (1879–1968). In 1944 Hahn was awarded the Nobel Prize for chemistry for discovering the process of nuclear fission together with Lise Meitner. In the early 1940s scientists in the United States used their discovery to develop the first atomic bomb.

Hahn arrived at McGill in 1905 from Berlin, Germany, and remained with Rutherford for about a

Ernest Rutherford is pictured here in 1906.

year. Many years later Hahn remembered the affection Rutherford's students felt for him: "Rutherford was so sincere and unassuming in his dealing with his students and with everyday things of life ... We had no doubt imagined that such a distinguished professor would be an unapproachable person, conscious of his dignity. Nothing could have been farther from the truth. I still possess a small photograph which shows him clearing away the snow from the entrance to his house. In this house were often evening guests, listening in rapt attention to the intimate piano-playing of Mrs. Rutherford or to the spirited narrative of the Professor."[10]

In July 1906 a review of Rutherford's work at McGill was published in the British science journal *Nature*. It described the relationship between the professor and his students: "Professor Rutherford inspires research students with some of his own enthusiasm and energy. He follows their results closely and is as delighted with any of their discoveries as with his own. He is generosity itself in giving a full measure of credit to those who do research work under his guidance."[11]

In 1906 Rutherford was offered the chance to return to England to a suitable position. (He had

*The home on Ste. Famille Street in Montreal, occupied by Rutherford
and his family from 1900 to 1907, as it appears today.*

already declined to apply for a position in London, a city he disliked, with a lab he considered unacceptable.) The professor of physics at Manchester University, Sir Arthur Schuster, was considering retiring. He would retire, however, only if Rutherford would agree to take his place. Rutherford was drawn to the offer mainly because Schuster had built the finest physics lab in England. Although it was not as well outfitted as the MPB at McGill, its facilities were much better than those even at the Cavendish. Rutherford wrote Schuster, "The fine laboratory you have built up is a great attraction to me as well as the opportunity of more scientific intercourse than occurs here."[12] After working out many details, Rutherford agreed to take up the position as head of the physics department at University of Manchester after finishing the academic year 1906–1907 at McGill. When J. J. Thomson heard a rumor to that effect, he wrote Rutherford: "I hope it is true. . . . It will be very delightful to have you back again."[13]

It was not without regret that Rutherford left Montreal. In submitting his resignation to McGill, he spoke of the "exceptional opportunities for carrying out my special scientific work" he had found at the MPB. He explained that "the determining factor" in his decision to take the new position was "my feeling that it is necessary to be in closer contact with European science than is possible on this side of the Atlantic."[14]

McGill University, too, regretted Rutherford's decision, and expressed its gratitude for all he had done during his time there: "In the course of nine years, crowded with epoch-making researches, Professor Rutherford has permanently associated the Macdonald Physics Laboratory with discoveries of such significance that their ultimate effect on the conception of the Physical Universe cannot yet be foretold."[15]

In May 1907 the Rutherfords moved to Manchester, England. Would the man who had written about eight papers a year in Montreal and come up with a revolutionary theory of matter be reduced now to sitting on his laurels?

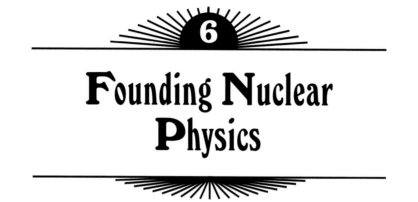

Founding Nuclear Physics

AS EARLY AS 1905 RUTHERFORD KNEW THAT his work was Nobel Prize material. In a letter to May in New Zealand (where she was on an extended visit with her mother), he wrote: "if I am to have a chance for a Nobel Prize in the next few years I must keep my work moving."[1]

It came as no great surprise to the scientific world that Rutherford was awarded a Nobel Prize in 1908 "for his investigations into the disintegration of the elements."[2] What surprised everyone, Rutherford included, was that he was honored with the prize not for physics but rather for chemistry. In December 1908 the Rutherfords traveled by boat to Stockholm, where the Swedish Royal Academy bestowed the honors. After Rutherford's health was toasted at the official banquet following the awards ceremony, he had a chance to make a few remarks. In a letter to her family in New Zealand, May reported, "Everyone says he made the speech of the evening and was rather amusing. He said he had dealt for a long time in transformations of varying length but that the quickest he had met was his own transformation in one moment from a physicist into a chemist!!"[3] (The official announcement had singled out Rutherford's work on the chemistry of radioactive substances and the disintegration of chemical elements.)

The following day the recipients of the award presented lectures discussing the significance of their work. In an address called "The Chemical Nature of the Alpha-Particles from Radioactive Substances," Rutherford spoke about his latest work at Manchester. As a research student at the Cavendish 10 years earlier, he had been the first to detect "alpha rays." His subsequent work had led him to observe that most minerals containing radioactive materials also contained unusually large amounts of the element helium. For a long time he had therefore suspected that alpha particles were actually atoms of helium. Each helium atom represented the decay of one radioactive atom, which threw out this less massive bit. At Manchester he had finally conclusively identified alpha particles as helium atoms stripped of their electrons. The alpha particles therefore were high-speed, positively charged particles.

Alpha particles would provide the means to Rutherford's next great discovery. Very few scientists go on to do even greater work after winning the Nobel Prize. Such was the case with Rutherford, however. His fascination with alpha particles would be the key. He began to use alpha particles as probes to investigate the interior structure of the atom. Long before scientists began to use gigantic particle accelerators, or "atom smashers," Rutherford understood that the inside of the atom could be studied by shooting tiny energetic particles into matter.

The nervous young man who had come to Montreal in 1898, worried that he would not be able to direct the research of others, had nonetheless managed to put together a creditable school of researchers at Montreal. At Manchester, however, his school became legendary. Almost 50 years later, physicist Edward Andrade recalled his youthful experience at the "Manchester research school . . . at the height of its activity, full of characters from all parts of the world working with joy under the energetic and inspiring influence of the great man," all benefiting from "Rutherford's human touch and power of inspiring others."[4]

Rutherford made sure that each of the researchers had an interesting topic on which to work. He allowed them a lot of independence to run their own experiments. He checked up on each researcher regularly to make sure that all was proceeding smoothly. According to Andrade, "Rutherford was . . . the boisterous, enthusiastic, inspiring friend, undoubtedly the leader but in close community with the led, stimulating rather than commanding . . . his team."[5]

Nearly all the researchers in the lab called Rutherford "Papa" and did their best to avoid being scolded by him. As an early recruit at Manchester once observed, "even the laziest worker was bound to be infected with something of his interest and enthusiasm, or at worst to be imbued with a healthy desire to avert his active disapproval. . . . Newcomers soon learnt that the sight of Rutherford singing lustily 'Onward, Christian soldiers' . . . as he walked round the corridors was an indication that all was going well."[6]

An important figure in Rutherford's Manchester school was Dr. Hans Geiger (1882–1947). Geiger had left Germany in 1906 to work with Professor Schuster, the man who had invited Rutherford to succeed him. Geiger became famous for the device that bears his name. The Geiger counter is an instrument for measuring radioactivity. It clicks as it detects instances of radioactive decay, clicking more often in the presence of higher radioactivity. Rutherford, assisted by Geiger, originally developed this device as a means to detect individual alpha particles.

One of Geiger's responsibilities was to teach students the techniques for measuring radioactivity. One day in 1909 Geiger reported that Ernest Marsden, an undergraduate, was ready to do some research on his own. Rutherford responded, "See if you can get some effect of alpha particles directly reflected from a metal surface."[7] The ingenious method Marsden designed to do just that has recently been called one of "The Ten Most Beautiful Experiments in Science."[8]

Marsden shot alpha particles at thin sheets of foil. He placed detecting screens around the foil to see if some of the particles would bounce back off them at large angles instead of passing through. The screens lit up when hit by alpha particles.

The current model of the atom was based on J. J. Thomson's discovery of the electron. In Thomson's atomic model, negatively charged electrons circled in rings within a thin fog of positively charged material. Thomson's atom was uniformly positive

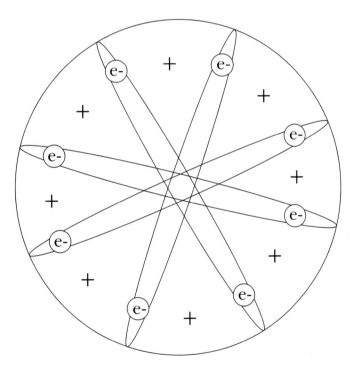

J. J. Thomson's model of the atom had negatively charged electrons circling in rings within a thin fog of positively charged material.

except for the electrons. If this model was correct, alpha particles should sail through the foil.

In Marsden's experiment, however, while most of the alpha particles passed through the foil, a few bounced straight back. Rutherford later described how surprised he was by the results of this "scattering" of alpha particles: "It was quite the most incredible event that has ever happened to me in my life. It was almost as incredible as if you had fired a 15-inch shell at a piece of tissue paper and it came back and hit you."[9] Eighty years later another scientist updated the comparison: "That under those circumstances an [alpha] particle would rebound at a large angle is as incredible as that a loaded Mack truck would veer back upon hitting a Volkswagen."[10] Rutherford had no immediate explanation for the results.

As he did other work over the course of the next two years, Rutherford continued to mull over the results of Marsden's research. In December 1910 he wrote an American colleague, "I think I can devise an atom much superior to J.J.'s."[11] Rutherford's new model of the atom consisted mainly of empty space. Such an atom would account for the fact that most of the alpha particles passed through the foil. Because like charges repel each other, he reasoned that whatever caused the positive alpha particles to bounce back also must have a positive charge. Only a strong electric force would cause the bouncing. Thus his new model of the atom contained a small, positively charged center, which he called the *nucleus*. Compared to electrons, the nucleus has a large mass. Rutherford compared his atomic model with the solar system. Just as planets orbit the sun in the solar system, electrons whirled around the nucleus.

Fifty years later a scientist in Rutherford's lab remembered being present at the "birth" of the atomic nucleus: "I remember two or three times at the laboratory teas hearing Rutherford say that there must be tremendous forces in the atom, and then he would leave it at that. But one of the great experiences of my life was that on one Sunday evening the Rutherfords had invited some of us to supper, and after supper the nuclear theory came out. . . . I also recollect that even on that first evening Rutherford was already speculating how small the nucleus might be."[12] Rutherford estimated that the nucleus was about 10,000 times smaller than the atom that contained it.

There was a problem with Rutherford's model of

the atom, however. If the electrons in his model obeyed the laws of physics, they should give off energy while circling the nucleus. As they gave off energy, the electrons should spiral inward and eventually collapse into the nucleus. If this were the case, the atoms that make up all matter would be totally unstable. The universe clearly consists of stable matter, however. As a result, Rutherford's new model was not immediately accepted. Within a few

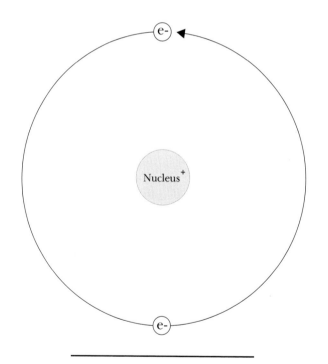

Rutherford's model of the atom proposed the existence of a positively charged nucleus containing the bulk of the particle's mass, around which the negatively charged electrons circled in rings.

years, however, the problem would be worked out, and a modified form of Rutherford's model would be endorsed by scientists everywhere.

The problem with the Rutherford atom was solved by a young Danish physicist, Niels Bohr. Bohr had received his doctorate in Copenhagen in spring 1911. He had been given a grant to support him while he did postdoctoral work abroad. Because the subject of Bohr's doctoral thesis was the electron theory of metals, he had chosen to work with the man who had discovered the electron. While J. J. Thomson had been a wonderful mentor for Rutherford, Bohr's experience was different. For a variety of reasons, Bohr found his work at the Cavendish unrewarding.

In December 1911 Bohr was impressed by Rutherford's jovial manner at the annual dinner at the Cavendish, which they both attended. Either just before or just after the festive dinner, Bohr was formally introduced to Rutherford by a physiology professor at the University of Manchester. Bohr's father, who had recently died, had been a professor of physiology in Copenhagen, and the Manchester professor had studied with him.

In early 1912 Bohr wrote Rutherford to inquire

about the possibility of spending the rest of his postdoctoral stay at Manchester. Half a century later Bohr recalled that Rutherford "said I should be welcome, but I had to settle with Thomson. He wouldn't take any student away from Thomson. . . . I just said to Thomson that I had only a year now in England and should be glad also to know something about radioactivity."[13]

On March 18, 1912, Rutherford wrote an American colleague, "Bohr, a Dane, has pulled out of Cambridge and turned up here to get some experience in radioactive work."[14] Bohr was not enthusiastic about the experiment Rutherford assigned him to carry out, but he thrived in Manchester all the same. As Bohr later reminisced, "Although Rutherford was always intensely occupied with the progress of his own work, he had the patience to listen to every young man, when he felt he had any idea, however modest, on his mind."[15]

Rutherford was soon to learn just how far Bohr's idea was from modest. When Bohr told Rutherford that he had some thoughts about how to solve the problem with the Rutherford model of the atom, Rutherford gave him permission to put aside the lab work. Bohr devoted the rest of his time in England to working out his variation on the atomic model.

In three major papers published in 1913, Bohr suggested that electrons do not fall into the nucleus because they can move around the nucleus only in certain fixed paths. According to Bohr, each path is a certain distance from the nucleus. Electrons in those paths, which are called energy levels, have

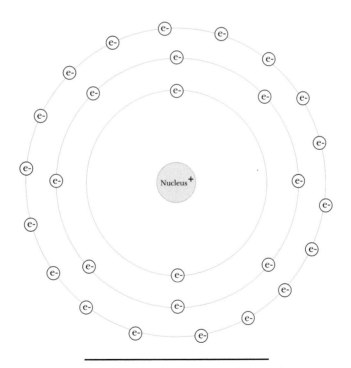

Bohr's model of the atom proposed that negatively charged electrons circled the positively charged nucleus in different levels. The first level outside the nucleus could contain a maximum of two electrons; the second level eight electrons; and the third level eighteen.

only certain amounts of energy. As long as an electron remains in one energy level, it gives off no energy. Bohr assumed that an atom gained or lost energy only when an electron moved from one level to another.

At first there was no experimental proof for Bohr's explanation of why the atom remained stable. Bohr was a theoretical physicist—one who tries to explain the behavior of matter in terms of basic laws. Rutherford was an experimental physicist—one who collects and interprets data about the behavior of matter, thereby giving theorists something to explain. Rutherford often made fun of "our theoretical friends," as he called them.[16] He once joked that while the theoreticians "play games with their symbols, . . . we . . . turn out the real solid facts of Nature."[17] But Rutherford understood the value of Bohr's contribution to his atomic model. In 1923 Rutherford expressed his admiration for Bohr's theoretical explanation for Rutherford's atomic model: "A radical departure from accepted views seemed essential if progress were to be made. . . . But the test of any theory is its power to suggest new relations, and in this respect Bohr's theory was triumphant from the first."[18]

Although in the years that followed, other scientists refined the Rutherford-Bohr model of the atom in a variety of ways, it continues to underlie our understanding of matter and energy. As one scientist has said, "Rutherford's nuclear theory of the atom . . . changed the whole face of modern physics."[19]

In 1914 Rutherford was knighted by King George V of England. The new Sir Ernest Rutherford was a little hesitant about the honor. He wrote a colleague at McGill, "I feel such forms of recognition are not very suitable to people like myself. However, I am, of course, pleased at this public recognition of my labours, and hope that my activity will not be lessened by this transformation."[20]

To another colleague he wrote about the reaction of his daughter to his honor, and to the fact that her parents would have to dress up appropriately to meet the king: "Eileen . . . is of the opinion that neither of her parents has the 'swank' and natural dignity for such decorations."[21]

Rutherford soon had the chance to prove how valuable his work was to his country. In August 1914 Germany invaded Belgium. As a result, Britain declared war on Germany. The Great War, which

Ernest Rutherford and Niels Bohr are seated on a bench while May Rutherford, Rosa Oliphant, and Margrethe Bohr (left to right) relax on the lawn.

would later be known as World War I, did not end until November 1918. Nearly 10 million troops died and about 21 million soldiers were wounded. At the outset of the war, the main combatants on one side were France, Britain, and Russia, known as the Allies. They opposed the Central Powers, made up of Germany and Austria-Hungary. In 1917 the United States joined the Allies.

When the war broke out Rutherford was on his way to a meeting in Australia of the British Association for the Advancement of Science. He stuck to his planned itinerary, however, and visited family in New Zealand and colleagues in Canada before returning to Manchester in January 1915.

The lab to which he returned was very different from the one he had left months earlier. Nearly fifty years later a young researcher at Manchester remembered the war's impact on the lab: "The coming of the war in August 1914 naturally broke up completely the family life, for such it was, of the laboratory. The majority of laboratory workers were dispersed and Rutherford's attention was diverted to problems of national importance."[22]

Developments during the first stages of the war convinced the British government for the first time that scientists could assist the military. For example, on May 7, 1915, a German submarine torpedoed and sank the *Lusitania*, a British cargo and passenger ship. Rutherford was asked to help improve the safety of Allied ships by protecting them from German submarines. For nearly two decades he had focused exclusively on radioactivity and atomic structure. Now, without hesitation, he was able to turn his attention to the laws of physics that shed light on how a submarine could be detected under water. He believed that the sounds submarines give off underwater were the best means to detect them—better, for example, than the heat they give off or their effects on the Earth's magnetic field. When the United States entered the war in 1917, Rutherford led the Allied delegation to Washington that communicated the newest advances in submarine detection.

Rutherford was one of two main inventors of the sonar method for using sound energy to detect and locate objects submerged in water. The other inventor was French physicist Paul Langevin (1872–1946). Langevin and Rutherford had been friends since 1895, when both were foreign research students at the Cavendish. The two men, however, did not collaborate in the development of sonar. After the war some of Rutherford's colleagues heard that Langevin took credit for developing the sonar method. They urged Rutherford to put forth his own claim. In typically modest fashion, Rutherford said, "If Langevin says he did it first, that's good enough . . . , let Langevin have the credit."[23]

Whenever the opportunity presented itself for some private research, Rutherford continued work bombarding gases with alpha particles. By the time the war was over, he had succeeded in splitting the atom in this manner. By doing so, he proved conclusively that the atom can be broken down into smaller particles. By 1917 Rutherford had figured out that he was able to smash an atomic nucleus, thereby changing one element into another. By bombarding nitrogen atoms with alpha particles, he was able to turn them into oxygen atoms.

Fifteen years earlier he and Soddy had figured out that nature had provided for one element to transform itself into another through the process of radioactivity. Now Rutherford was able to control the transformation of one element into another by using the alpha particle, a product of natural radioactivity. According to Bohr, this achievement of Rutherford's "in the course of time was to give rise to such tremendous consequences as regards man's mastery of the forces of nature."[24]

By the time the results of Rutherford's bombardment experiments were published, he had transferred his home base yet again, for the final time. For the last stage of his career Rutherford was based at the Cavendish Laboratory. There he had been the first to detect alpha particles in 1898. Then he had been a research student in the director's lab. Now he was to become director of that lab himself.

Rutherford wrote his mother about his decision to move back to Cambridge: "It was a difficult question to decide whether to leave Manchester as they have been very good to me, but I felt it probably best for me to come here, for after all it is the chief physics chair in the country and has turned out most of the physics professors of the last twenty years. It will of course be a wrench, pulling up my roots again and starting afresh to make new friends, but fortunately I know a good few people here already."[25]

Scientific Statesman

A SCIENTIST WHO SPENT THE YEAR 1913–14 with Rutherford recalled many years later, "At Manchester the cares of office sat lightly on him and he revelled in the free exercise of his full creative powers."[1] At the Cavendish, however, things were different. In the last stage of his career, Rutherford spent less time as a creative scientist in his own right and more time as a statesman of science. He held many official positions that required him to spend time away from Cambridge and the lab.

For example, as president of the Royal Society from 1925 to 1930 he had to make regular trips to London. Once he became Lord Rutherford of Nelson in 1931, he made occasional addresses on the role of science in the national economy to the House of Lords, of which he was now a member. Despite these commitments that kept him away from the Cavendish, Rutherford continued to find time to direct a number of students into brilliant careers, oversee the shift from "small science" to "big science," and become involved in foreign affairs on behalf of other scientists. One of the winners of the 1979 Nobel Prize for physics has remarked that if Rutherford's "work at McGill, Manchester, and Cambridge were divided among three different men, they could each be said to have had unusually productive careers in science."[2]

Following the war, the Cavendish Laboratory was in need of rejuvenating. Rutherford provided just the right kind of guidance. As Bohr said in 1926, Rutherford was leading his researchers in "a vigorous campaign to deprive the atoms of their secrets by all the means at the disposal of modern science."[3] He seems to have decided soon after making the move from Manchester that it was time to pass the scientific mantle. James Chadwick, a researcher whom Rutherford asked to join him at the Cavendish, later remembered being told by Rutherford on more than one occasion, "I have done enough for one man; it is now the task of the younger generation to tackle the problems about the structure of the nucleus." According to Chadwick, "This was perhaps the first time that a great laboratory had concentrated so large a part of its effort on one particular problem."[4]

Rutherford put Chadwick in charge of supervising the lab and the research students. Chadwick was also one of the brilliant researchers inspired by Rutherford's work.

In June 1920 Rutherford gave, for the second time in his life, the Bakerian Lecture to the Royal Society. In his 1904 Bakerian he had presented the foundations of the science of radioactivity. In the later lecture he explained in detail the last research he had carried out at Manchester: he had bombarded the nitrogen nucleus with alpha particles, driving out a hydrogen nucleus. (Later that summer Rutherford suggested calling the hydrogen nucleus the "proton." The scientific community adopted the name for the positively charged particle found in all nuclei.) What remained after the hydrogen nucleus escaped was no longer nitrogen. He had succeeded in using alpha particles to transform one element into another. (Rutherford's experiment added two protons from the alpha particle to the nitrogen, but one proton was emitted, making a net gain of one proton. Thus the nitrogen was transmuted into oxygen, the next element in the periodic table.)

In the 1920 Bakerian Lecture, Rutherford also made a prediction that would, over a decade later, guide his colleague Chadwick into a Nobel Prize for physics. "It seems very likely," Rutherford said, that there is "an atom of mass 1 which has zero nuclear charge"—in other words, a particle about as massive as the proton but having no electric charge.[5]

Rutherford began suggesting experiments to his research students to uncover the neutron, but nothing turned up for over a decade.

Interestingly enough, the experiment that finally led Chadwick in 1932 to detect the neutron was inspired not by Rutherford but by Marie Curie's daughter and son-in-law. Just as Marie and Pierre Curie had been a productive husband-and-wife research team, their older daughter, Irène, and her husband, Frédéric Joliot-Curie, were likewise a "power couple" among physics researchers. The Joliot-Curies would share the 1935 Nobel Prize in chemistry for their discovery of artificial radioactivity. That achievement was inspired by Rutherford's technique of alpha-particle bombardment of nuclei. Because the

Joliot-Curies had never read Rutherford's 1920 Bakerian Lecture, however, they missed out on the discovery of the neutron that led Chadwick to the Nobel Prize in physics that same year.

Chadwick repeated an experiment described by the Joliot-Curies, who had bombarded the element beryllium with alpha particles. The Joliot-Curies had not known what to make of the unknown radiation that it released. Chadwick, however, identified the radiation as being composed of particles of mass approximately equal to that of the proton, but without electrical charge. In other words, he had detected a new subatomic particle—the neutron. The Joliot-Curies regretted their belief that in lectures like the Bakerian "it is rare to find anything novel which has not been published elsewhere."[6]

Chadwick's discovery of the neutron provided a new tool to replace alpha particles as probes for studying the nucleus. Since neutrons lacked electric charge, they could penetrate the nucleus more effectively than alpha particles, whose positive electric charge led to their being deflected.

Another brilliant colleague at the Cavendish was the Russian engineer Peter Kapitza (1894–1984). Rutherford had been dead for over forty years when

Kapitza won the Nobel Prize in 1978 for inventions and discoveries in low-temperature physics. Nonetheless, the Russian owed a lot to Rutherford's early interest in him. The interaction between Rutherford and Kapitza also helped bring about the transition from "little science" to "big science."

When Kapitza came to England in 1921, he had already trained as an electrical engineer in Russia. Although the Cavendish was overcrowded and Rutherford had turned away several researchers interested in working there, Kapitza charmed his way into the Cavendish. After being trained there in radioactivity, Kapitza studied properties of particles emitted by radioactive nuclei. He used an apparatus designed at the Cavendish called a cloud chamber along with a magnet that bent the paths of the charged particles. Soon, however, he became more interested in the magnets themselves than in the charged particles. To the astonishment of everyone else at the Cavendish, Kapitza talked Rutherford into finding the money for a very expensive magnetic research lab within the Cavendish.

Everyone knew that Rutherford was a "sealing wax and string" kind of physicist who insisted on using the cheapest materials possible for an experiment. Rutherford understood, however, that the electrical and magnetic equipment Kapitza needed could help reveal further secrets of nature—for example, how matter behaves at very low temperatures. Rutherford also understood that the equipment could be made more easily and cheaply by industry than by hand. In 1925 Rutherford was elected president of the prestigious Royal Society. Four years later he became the chairman of the government's Department of Scientific and Industrial Research (DSIR) Advisory Council. His requests for funding from the government and from the Royal Society, therefore, had a lot of influence.

By summer 1930 Rutherford had obtained over 16,000 pounds for Kapitza's lab from the DSIR—a sum greater than the entire Cavendish research budget. Before the end of 1930, he had also helped get a grant of 15,000 pounds from the Royal Society for the University of Cambridge to build and equip a lab for Kapitza's research. The Royal Society Mond Laboratory, located in the courtyard of the Cavendish, was opened in 1933. Kapitza was named its director.

Rutherford had no son of his own, and various younger scientists over the years developed a

Rutherford in his lab, circa 1926.

father-son relationship with him. Bohr, for example, later said of Rutherford, "To me he had almost been like a second father."[7] Kapitza also had for Rutherford the affection, tinged with awe, of a son. In October 1925, when Rutherford was on a trip to New Zealand, Kapitza wrote him, "We are missing you very much. I feel myself very uncomfortably as nobody is scolding me sometimes a little."[8]

Rutherford soon became known around the Cavendish by Kapitza's pet name for him: "the Crocodile." Kapitza once explained the name in this way: "In Russia the crocodile is the symbol for the father of the family and it is also regarded with awe and admiration because it has a stiff neck and cannot turn back. It just goes straight forward with gaping jaws—like science, like Rutherford."[9] On another occasion Kapitza told Chadwick that he was always afraid that Rutherford would bite off his head, like a crocodile, while they were discussing physics.[10] In any case, without Rutherford's knowledge, Kapitza had a well-known sculptor carve a crocodile into the brick wall near the entrance to the Mond Laboratory. Kapitza also commissioned the same sculptor, Eric Gill, to make a sculpture of Rutherford for the entrance hall.

Unlike other Russian expatriates, Kapitza was not living abroad because he hated the Communists who had formed the Soviet Union in the aftermath of the Russian Revolution of 1917. He supported the Soviet Union's professed goals of economic and social progress. From 1926 on, Kapitza routinely visited Russia nearly every year, often at the invitation of high-ranking Communists. It took him and everyone else by surprise when the Russian government informed him in summer 1934 that the Soviet Union required his scientific abilities. He would thus not be permitted to return to England.

Rutherford had never been one for political involvement, but Kapitza's case drew him into urgent correspondence with various Soviet officials. It eventually became clear that the efforts of Rutherford and other scientists would not succeed in persuading the Soviet government to release Kapitza. The Soviet Embassy in London released a statement in April 1935 saying, "Cambridge would no doubt like to have all the world's greatest scientists in its laboratories in much the same way as the Soviet would like to have Lord Rutherford and other of your great physicists in her laboratories. The plain fact is that Professor Kapitza is a Soviet citizen and his country needs him."[11]

Rutherford arranged to sell the Soviets the equipment that had been installed for Kapitza's use at the Mond and encouraged Kapitza to get back to work. The Soviet Union built the Institute for Physical Problems for Kapitza, where he went on to establish a research school worthy of his old mentor, Rutherford.

The Kapitza incident was not Rutherford's only

involvement either in "big science" or in foreign affairs. Rutherford was able to open up the study of nuclear reactions with the equivalent of "sealing wax and string"—he used alpha particles from a natural radioactive source. Soon after he opened up this avenue of research, however, it became clear that "big science" would be a much better way to proceed. As Bohr wrote in 1961, "Although much important new evidence was obtained in these investigations, it was more and more felt that, for a broader attack on nuclear problems, the natural alpha-ray sources were not sufficient. . . ." Chadwick urged Rutherford to build a particle accelerator at the Cavendish. According to Bohr, Rutherford, who "hitherto had achieved with the help of very modest experimental equipment" such fine results, was at first "reluctant to embark upon such a great and expensive enterprise in his laboratory."[12] But when Rutherford became convinced that the expense would pay off in better results, he agreed. By spring 1932, the Cavendish had a fine particle accelerator. With it, two of Rutherford's colleagues, John Cockcroft and Ernest Walton, split the atom using very high speed protons. With Rutherford's blessing, the age of "big science" had truly begun. Today's accelerators produce and

Rutherford continued to work on scientific problems and remained active in the scientific community throughout his life.

precisely control beams more numerous and energetic than the alpha particles naturally emitted from a radioactive source.

Even before Rutherford tried to intervene with the Soviet government on behalf of Kapitza, he had become involved with foreign affairs. On January 30, 1933, Adolf Hitler became chancellor of Germany. Shortly thereafter, the Nazi regime proclaimed racial laws that barred Jews from holding public positions. University professors and researchers working in German institutes were included. Many of Germany's physicists were Jewish. Rutherford was at the forefront of scientists who tried to assist their displaced German colleagues. About 1600 professors and research students were affected. According to Rutherford's younger colleague Mark Oliphant, "Rutherford was appalled by this brutality, especially as the greatest of the German scientists, some of whom had worked with him and many of whom he knew intimately, were among the victims."[13]

Within a few months, Rutherford became head of a newly formed organization, the Academic Assistance Council (later called the Society for the Protection of Science and Learning). Rutherford chaired a large public meeting on October 3, 1933, aimed at raising money to support Germans ousted from their positions. The main speaker was Albert Einstein, the most famous German scientist.

The problem facing Rutherford's organization and others like it was not simple. England and the rest of the world were in the midst of the Great Depression, the worst and longest period of high unemployment and low business activity in modern times. The idea that a position might go to a refugee scientist instead of an English one did not sit well with everyone. Rutherford's efforts to help his German colleagues resulted in some hate mail. Nonetheless, by the time of his death, he had helped find permanent positions for 507 refugees and temporary spots for another 308.

As the 1930s went on, Rutherford grew busier than ever. According to an article published in 1936, about the time he turned sixty-five, "He wears his years very lightly and vigorously. He has no time to worry about such little things as growing old. He is too much absorbed with the present."[14] There was no particular reason to think he would not go on with amazing energy for many more years. His father, James, had died in 1928 at age eighty-nine. His mother, Martha, had died in 1935 at age ninety-two. True, Rutherford was deeply shaken when his only child, Eileen, had died in December 1930 at the age of twenty-nine. Eileen, who was married to a mathematical physicist at the Cavendish, Ralph Fowler, had recently delivered the fourth of Rutherford's grandchildren. Rutherford was able to deal with some of his grief, however, by doting on the Fowler children.

It was also true that Rutherford suffered from a slight hernia, or rupture, near his belly button. In this type of hernia, a portion of the bowel sticks out through the muscular wall of the abdomen. The danger of abdominal hernia is that the muscles of the abdomen may contract. The contraction, in turn, can choke off the part of the bowel that protrudes. If this kind of strangulated hernia develops, surgery is required immediately.

Rutherford's hernia normally caused no problems, although he wore a truss—a pad supported by a belt—to keep the bowel inside the abdominal wall. On Thursday, October 14, 1937, Rutherford felt ill. He was operated on for strangulated hernia the following night. Although he seemed to be recovering normally, he died the following Tuesday evening, October 19, 1937. He was only sixty-six.

A number of Rutherford's closest colleagues,

including Bohr and Mark Oliphant, learned of his death by telegraph early the next morning while at a meeting in Bologna, Italy. According to Oliphant, "When the meeting for that morning assembled, Bohr went to the front, and with faltering voice and tears in his eyes informed the gathering of what had happened. Bohr went on to give a short address about Rutherford, which was one of the most moving experiences of my life. He spoke from his heart of the debt which science owed so great a man whom he was privileged to call both his master and his friend."[15]

Rutherford's ashes were buried in London's Westminster Abbey. Among the remains of other great British scientists nearby are those of J. J. Thomson, who died three years after the former research student who became his successor at the Cavendish.

Rutherford died without knowing the far-reaching effects his work would have. In 1963, Rutherford's younger colleague Edward Andrade said, "I think it was well for his peace of mind that he did not foresee the terrors, the threat to the human race, that would grow directly from the work of his school, for the nuclear bomb derives directly from the early experiments on the disruption of the nucleus, which in their turn derived from his Manchester work."[16]

Rutherford would surely take pleasure, however, in other outcomes of his work. Steven Weinberg, who shared the 1979 Nobel Prize for physics, reminds us that the alpha-particle technique Rutherford used to discover the atomic nucleus has been repeated countless times since that 1911 discovery. For example, in 1968 a group of scientists at the Stanford Linear Accelerator shot a beam of high-energy electrons to probe the inside of the proton. "It is believed that the small heavy particle found in this way inside the proton is a quark."[17] Quarks are examples of elementary particles, which have no known smaller parts. Quarks make up one of three families of particles that serve as "building blocks" of matter. So not only the atomic nucleus but also an even more elementary particle of matter was discovered using Rutherford's bombardment technique.

A modern version of that technique is called Rutherford Backscattering Spectrometry (RBS) in his honor. RBS is used to identify the elements in a sample. It has proven very helpful in exploring our solar system. Long before the first astronauts went to the Moon, RBS on robotic spacecraft was used to identify and measure what elements were on its surface. Later, in 1997, RBS was used to send back to Earth information about the elements on the surface of Mars. The technique also has important uses in the micro-electronics industry, where it can find defects in very thin multi-layered structures. It even has life-saving potential. Medical researchers hope that RBS may enable them to cure a fatal disease caused by too much iron in cells.

Rather than a legacy of terror and threat, Rutherford's scientific legacy continues to be one of enthusiastic discovery and hope for the future. Rutherford's belief that scientific ingenuity can trick nature into revealing its deepest secrets continues to inspire 21st-century researchers in many fields.

Activities

Activity One: Electromagnets

Rutherford's first research was in the field of electricity and magnetism. In 1820 a Danish physics teacher, Hans Christian Oersted, discovered accidentally that electric currents produce magnetic fields. Seven years later an American physicist, Joseph Henry, built on this discovery by inventing a practical electromagnet. An electromagnet is a coil that is magnetized by an electric current passing through it. Electromagnets are useful because their magnetism can be switched on and off. The purpose of this activity is to identify the variables that affect the strength of an electromagnet.

Materials needed:

- Two 1.5-volt dry cells
- Insulated wire, with stripped ends
- A switch
- A large nail
- Small metal objects, such as
  paper clips or tacks

Procedure:

PART A

1. Wind 10 turns of wire around the large nail. Do not overlap them.

2. Connect one dry cell terminal to one switch terminal with wire.

3. Connect one end of the coil's wire to the dry cell and the other end to the switch. *NOTE: The current in this circuit is too weak to harm you.*

4. Close the switch and try to pick up some small metal objects with the large nail. Record how many you can pick up.

5. Open the switch. Observe and record what happens to the objects.

PART B

1. Repeat steps 1–5 with 25 turns of wire around the nail.

2. Record how many objects you can pick up. Then open the switch and disconnect the wires.

PART C

1. Connect both dry cells by attaching a wire from one center terminal to the end terminal on the other cell.

2. Connect a second wire from the other terminal of a cell to the switch.

3. Connect one end of the electromagnet from Part B to the remaining cell terminal. *NOTE: The current in this circuit is too weak to harm you.*

4. Close the switch, and try to pick up paper clips or tacks.

5. Record how many objects you can pick up.

6. Open the switch, disconnect the wires, and unwind the electromagnet.

Analysis and Conclusions

1. What does the switch do to the electromagnet?

2. What factors affect the strength of the electromagnet?

3. Did you pick up the greatest number of objects in Part A, B, or C?

Activity Two: Making a Half-Life Model

While they were at McGill University, Rutherford and Frederick Soddy developed the theory of radioactive decay, including the concept of half-life. They determined that every radioactive atom has a specific half-life. The purpose of this activity is to demonstrate that radioactive decay takes place at a predictable rate.

Materials needed:
- 100 light-colored beans
- A shoe box and lid
- A felt-tip marker
- A pencil
- Some graph paper

Procedure and Observations:

PART A

1. Use the marker to put an "X" on one side of each bean. The beans represent radioactive atoms.

2. Put the beans in the box and place the lid on the box.

3. Shake the box for a few seconds. Remove the lid and take out the beans that are "X" side up.

4. Count the beans that remain in the box and record this number.

5. Repeat this procedure four more times. Be sure to count and record the number of beans that are left each time. Each counting represents one half-life.

PART B

1. Make a graph plotting "Beans remaining" on the vertical axis and "Number of times beans counted" on the horizontal axis. On

the vertical axis mark off 10 squares. Label the bottom one 0. Then mark 20, 40, 60, 80, and 100 on every other square. On the horizontal axis mark off five squares and label them 0 to 5.

2. Include a dot at the 100 mark on the vertical axis. This dot represents the 100 beans you had in the box at the beginning of the activity. Enter your five bean counts in the proper places on the graph.

3. Draw a line connecting the six points marked on the graph.

Analysis and Conclusions

1. About what fraction of the 100 beans remained in the box after each count? Remember to base each of your fractions on 100 beans.

2. Suppose 250,000 years passed each time the beans were counted, and each bean represents the very rare form of uranium mentioned in Chapter 5. Let the box with 100 beans represent a rock. If the rock contained 25 "beans" when it was found, how long ago was it formed?

Chronology

1871—Ernest Rutherford born in Nelson, New Zealand, on August 30.

1890—Rutherford begins studying at Canterbury College, University of New Zealand, Christchurch, on a New Zealand Junior Scholarship.

1892—Rutherford completes his B.A. degree.

1893—Rutherford completes his M.A. degree with first class honors in mathematics and mathematical physics, and in physical science.

1894—Rutherford completes his B.Sc. degree.

1895—Rutherford is awarded an Exhibition of 1851 Scholarship and goes as a research student to the Cavendish Laboratory of the University of Cambridge, England.

1897—Rutherford earns a second B.A. from the University of Cambridge.

1898—Rutherford discovers and names alpha and beta radiation. He becomes a professor of physics at McGill University, Montreal, Canada.

1900—Rutherford marries Mary (May) Georgina Newton in New Zealand and returns with his wife to Montreal.

1901—University of New Zealand grants Rutherford a D.Sc. Eileen Rutherford, the only child of May and Ernest, is born.

1903—Rutherford and Frederick Soddy publish their theory of radioactive decay. Rutherford is elected a Fellow of the Royal Society.

1904—Rutherford publishes his first book, *Radioactivity*; gives the Bakerian Lecture to the Royal Society; and uses the theory of radioactive decay to estimate the age of the earth.

1907—Rutherford becomes professor of physics at the University of Manchester, England; assisted by Hans Geiger, he develops the Rutherford-Geiger detector to detect individual alpha particles.

1908—Rutherford receives the Nobel Prize for Chemistry "for his investigations into the disintegration of the elements, and the chemistry of radioactive substances."

1911—Rutherford discovers the nuclear structure of the atom from the behavior displayed by alpha particles shot through thin gold foil.

1913—Rutherford publishes *Radioactive Substances and Their Radiations.*

1914—Rutherford is knighted. World War I begins.

1915—Rutherford begins war work to help detect enemy submarines.

1917—Rutherford transforms nitrogen into oxygen by alpha particle bombardment, thus becoming the first to cause the artificial disintegration of a stable nucleus.

1919—Rutherford is appointed director of the Cavendish Laboratory and professor at the University of Cambridge.

1920—Rutherford proposes that the hydrogen nucleus be called the proton. In his Bakerian Lecture he predicts the existence of the neutron.

1925—Rutherford is elected president of the Royal Society.

1930—Rutherford's daughter dies shortly after giving birth to his fourth grandchild.

1931—Rutherford is raised to the peerage and becomes Lord Rutherford of Nelson, with a seat in the House of Lords.

1932—James Chadwick, Rutherford's colleague and former student, discovers the neutron predicted by Rutherford in 1920. The Cavendish particle accelerator uses artificially accelerated protons to split the atom.

1933—Rutherford becomes president of the Academic Assistance Council and works to find positions and funding for refugee scholars from Nazi Germany.

1934—Rutherford intervenes unsuccessfully with Soviet authorities on behalf of Peter Kapitza.

1937—Rutherford dies on October 19.

1955—McGill University creates the Rutherford Chair in Physics.

1967—The Rutherford Museum at McGill University, containing a collection of the actual apparatus Rutherford used there, is officially opened.

1991—The site of Rutherford's birth near Nelson is turned into the Rutherford Birthplace, where visitors can learn about his life and work.

1992—A portrait of Rutherford from 1914 is placed on the $100 New Zealand note.

1997—Element 104 is named rutherfordium (Rf) in Rutherford's honor; Rutherford Backscattering Spectrometry is used to identify elements on the surface of Mars.

2001—A visitors' center is opened in the Rutherford Den, where Rutherford carried out his research at Canterbury College.

2003—The Pickering/Rutherford/Havelock Memorial is opened at Havelock, New Zealand, to commemorate the achievements of Rutherford and of New Zealand-born William H. Pickering (1910–2004), who led the effort that placed the first U.S. satellite into Earth orbit in 1958, and ushered in the era of robotic space exploration.

Chapter Notes

Chapter 1. A Scholarship He Almost Did Not Win

1. John Campbell, *Rutherford: Scientist Supreme* (Christchurch, New Zealand: AAS Publications, 1999), p.192.

2. David Wilson, *Rutherford: Simple Genius* (Cambridge, MA: MIT Press, 1983), p. 23.

3. Campbell, p. 382.

Chapter 2. Loss and Luck

1. A. S. Eve, *Rutherford: Being the Life and Letters of the Rt. Hon. Lord Rutherford, O.M.* (New York: Macmillan; and Cambridge, England: Cambridge University Press, 1939), p. 2.

2. Cecil Leonard Boltz, *The Great Nobel Prizes: Ernest Rutherford* (Geneva: Heron Books, 1970), p. 12.

3. John Campbell, *Rutherford: Scientist Supreme* (Christchurch, New Zealand: AAS Publications, 1999), p. 319.

4. Ibid., p.197.

5. Eve, p. 4.

6. Campbell, p. 64.

7. John Rowland, *Ernest Rutherford: Atom Pioneer* (New York: Philosophical Library, 1957), p. 15.

Chapter 3. Research and Romance

1. A. S. Eve, *Rutherford: Being the Life and Letters of the Rt. Hon. Lord Rutherford, O.M.* (New York: Macmillan; and Cambridge, England: Cambridge University Press, 1939), p. 10.

2. John Campbell, *Rutherford: Scientist Supreme* (Christchurch, New Zealand: AAS Publications, 1999), p. 107.

3. Ibid., p. 98.

4. Ibid., p. 119.

5. David Wilson, *Rutherford: Simple Genius* (Cambridge, MA: MIT Press, 1983), p. 45.

6. Eve, p. 8.

7. Campbell, p. 146.

8. Ibid., p. 158.

9. Ibid., p. 166.

10. Ibid., p. 173.

11. Ibid., p. 189.

12. Ibid., p. 128.

13. Ibid., p. 184.

14. Ibid., p. 209.

Chapter 4. From Radio to Radioactivity

1. A. S. Eve, *Rutherford: Being the Life and Letters of the Rt. Hon. Lord Rutherford, O.M.* (New York: Macmillan; and Cambridge, England: Cambridge University Press, 1939), p. 13.

2. Ibid., p. 15.

3. Sir J. J. Thomson, *Recollections and Reflections* (New York: Macmillan, 1937), p. 137.

4. Ivor B. N. Evans, *Man of Power: The Life Story of Baron Rutherford of Nelson* (London, England: The Scientific Book Club, 1939), p. 35.

5. Eve, p. 20.

6. Richard Rhodes, *The Making of the Atomic Bomb* (New York: Simon and Schuster, 1986), p. 38.

7. Cecil Leonard Boltz, *The Great Nobel Prizes: Ernest Rutherford* (Geneva: Heron Books, 1970), p. 45.

8. Eve, p. 26.

9. John Campbell, *Rutherford: Scientist Supreme* (Christchurch, New Zealand: AAS Publications, 1999), p. 220.

10. Sir J. J. Thomson, p. 411.

11. Norman Feather, *Lord Rutherford* (Glasgow: Blackie & Son, 1940; London, England: Priory Press Limited, 1973), p. 46.

12. Campbell, p. 248.

13. Eve, p. 55.

14. Ibid., p. 53.

15. Ibid., p. 56.

16. Ibid., p. 54.

17. Boltz, p. 59.

Chapter 5. The Mysteries of Radioactivity

1. David Wilson, *Rutherford: Simple Genius* (Cambridge, MA: MIT Press, 1983), p. 147.

2. Ibid., p. 163.

3. John Campbell, *Rutherford: Scientist Supreme* (Christchurch, New Zealand: AAS Publications, 1999), p. 263.

4. A. S. Eve, *Rutherford: Being the Life and Letters of the Rt. Hon. Lord Rutherford, O.M.* (New York: Macmillan; and Cambridge, England: Cambridge University Press, 1939), p. 71.

5. Wilson, p. 147.

6. Ibid., p. 197.

7. Eve, p. 116.

8. "Welcome," *The Royal Institution of Great Britain,* 2002 <http://www.rigb.org/> (May 27, 2004).

9. Eve, p. 107.

10. Ibid., pp. 142–143.

11. Ibid., pp. 139–140.

12. Wilson, p. 217.

13. Ibid., pp. 220–221.

14. Ibid., p. 222.

15. Eve, p. 155.

Chapter 6. Founding Nuclear Physics

1. A. S. Eve, *Rutherford: Being the Life and Letters of the Rt. Hon. Lord Rutherford, O.M.* (New York: Macmillan; and Cambridge, England: Cambridge University Press, 1939), p. 127.

2. "The Nobel Prize in Chemistry 1908," *Nobel e-Museum*, November 20, 2003, <http://www.nobel.se/chemistry/laureates/1908/> (May 27, 2004).

3. John Campbell, *Rutherford: Scientist Supreme* (Christchurch, New Zealand: AAS Publications, 1999), p. 317.

4. E. N. da C. Andrade, "Rutherford at Manchester, 1913–14," in J. B. Birks, ed., *Rutherford at Manchester* (New York: W. A. Benjamin, Inc., 1963), p. 27.

5. Ibid., p. 29.

6. H. R. Robinson, "Rutherford: Life and Work to the Year 1919, with Personal Reminiscences of the Manchester Period," in J. B. Birks, ed., *Rutherford at Manchester* (New York: W. A. Benjamin, Inc., 1963), pp. 76, 78.

7. Campbell, p. 332.

8. Robert P. Crease, *The Prism and the Pendulum: The Ten Most Beautiful Experiments in Science* (New York: Random House, 2003), pp. 169–183.

9. Richard Rhodes, *The Making of the Atomic Bomb* (New York: Simon and Schuster, 1986), p. 49.

10. Abraham Pais, *Niels Bohr's Times, in Physics, Philosophy, and Polity* (Oxford: Clarendon Press, 1991), p. 123.

11. Lawrence Badash, ed., *Rutherford and Boltwood: Letters on Radioactivity* (New Haven and London: Yale University Press, 1969), p. 235.

12. J. B. Birks, ed., *Rutherford at Manchester* (New York: W. A. Benjamin, Inc., 1963), pp. 18–19.

13. Niels Bohr, interview by Thomas Kuhn, November 1, 1962, p. 8. *Archives for the History of Quantum Physics, Niels Bohr Library,* American Institute of Physics, College Park, Md.

14. Badash, p. 265.

15. Niels Bohr, "Reminiscences of the Founder of Nuclear Science and of Some Developments Based on His Work," in J. B. Birks, ed., *Rutherford at Manchester* (New York: W. A. Benjamin, Inc., 1963), p. 116.

16. Mark Oliphant, *Rutherford: Recollections of the Cambridge Days* (Amsterdam, London, New York: Elsevier Publishing Company, 1972), p. 28.

17. Eve, p. 304.

18. David Wilson, *Rutherford: Simple Genius* (Cambridge, MA: MIT Press, 1983), p. 337.

19. H. R. Robinson, "Rutherford: Life and Work to the Year 1919, with Personal Reminiscences of the Manchester Period," in J. B. Birks, ed., Rutherford at Manchester (New York: W. A. Benjamin, Inc., 1963), p. 69.

20. Campbell, p. 347.

21. Wilson, p. 340.

22. E. N. da C. Andrade, "Rutherford at Manchester, 1913–14" in J. B. Birks, ed., *Rutherford at Manchester* (New York: W. A. Benjamin, Inc., 1963), p. 27.

23. Wilson, p. 373.

24. Niels Bohr, "Reminiscences of the Founder of Nuclear Science and of Some Developments Based on His Work," in J. B. Birks, ed., *Rutherford at Manchester* (New York: W. A. Benjamin, Inc., 1963), p. 140.

25. Wilson, p. 413.

Chapter 7. Scientific Statesman

1. E. N. da C. Andrade, "Rutherford at Manchester, 1913–14," in J. B. Birks, ed., *Rutherford at Manchester* (New York: W. A. Benjamin, Inc., 1963), p. 42.

2. Steven Weinberg, *The Discovery of Subatomic Particles* (Cambridge, England: Cambridge University Press, 2003), p. 99.

3. A. S. Eve, *Rutherford: Being the Life and Letters of the Rt. Hon. Lord Rutherford, O.M.* (New York and Cambridge, England: Macmillan and Cambridge University Press, 1939), p. 319.

4. James Chadwick, foreword, Mark Oliphant, *Rutherford: Recollections of the Cambridge Days* (Amsterdam, London, New York: Elsevier Publishing Company, 1972), p. x.

5. Eve, p. 281.

6. Ibid., p. 360.

7. Niels Bohr, "Reminiscences of the Founder of Nuclear Science and of Some Developments Based on His Work," *Proceedings of the Physical Society,* LXXVIII, 6, p. 1115.

8. Lawrence Badash, *Kapitza, Rutherford, and the Kremlin* (New Haven and London: Yale University Press, 1985), p. 18.

9. John Campbell, *Rutherford: Scientist Supreme* (Christchurch, New Zealand: AAS Publications, 1999), p. 388.

10. Mark Oliphant, *Rutherford: Recollections of the Cambridge Days* (Amsterdam, London, New York: Elsevier Publishing Company, 1972), p. 92.

11. Badash, p. 31.

12. Bohr, p. 1108.

13. Oliphant, p. 57.

14. Eve, pp. 416–417.

15. Oliphant, p. 155.

16. Andrade, pp. 41–42.

17. Weinberg, p. 123.

Glossary

alpha particle—Particle emitted by decaying radioactive nuclei, identified as a positively charged helium nucleus.

atom—Smallest bit of an element that has all the properties of that element.

beta particle—Particle emitted by decaying radioactive nuclei, identified as a rapidly moving electron.

daughter—Product of radioactive decay.

electromagnetic wave—Energy traveling through space as a result of changing electricity and magnetism.

electromagnetism—Theory that shows how electricity and magnetism result from a single force.

electron—Negatively charged particle orbiting the nucleus of an atom.

element—Any of the simplest substances of matter that cannot be decomposed by heat, light, or electricity.

energy level—One of the possible amounts of energy an electron may have in an atom.

experimentalist—A scientist who collects and interprets data about the behavior of matter, thereby giving theorists something to explain.

gamma ray—Energetic electromagnetic wave emitted during radioactive decay.

half-life—Time it takes for half the nuclei in a quantity of a radioactive substance to decay.

Nazis—Members of the antisemitic German political party that governed Germany from 1933 to the end of World War II.

neutron—Nuclear particle having no electric charge.

Nobel Prize—Prestigious award founded in 1901 for outstanding achievement in physics, chemistry, physiology or medicine, literature, and world peace. A sixth prize, for economic sciences, was added in 1969.

nucleus—Positively charged core of an atom.

parent—First radioactive atom to undergo radioactive decay in a radioactive series.

particle accelerator—Machine for speeding subatomic particles to high velocity; also called an atom-smasher.

proton—Name suggested by Rutherford in 1920 for the hydrogen nucleus and later accepted as the term for the positively charged particle found free or in a nucleus.

quark—Elementary particle discovered in 1968 using Rutherford's 1911 bombardment technique.

radioactivity—Spontaneous decay of a nucleus into a lighter nucleus, very tiny particles, and radiation.

Soviet Union—Union of 15 Communist-controlled republics formed under Russia's leadership in 1922 and dissolved in 1991.

theoretician—A scientist who tries to explain the behavior of matter in terms of basic laws.

wireless telegraphy—System of transmitting messages or signals over a distance by means of radio waves rather than through wires or cable.

Further Reading

Fox, Karen. *The Chain Reaction: Pioneers of Nuclear Science*. Danbury, Conn.: Franklin Watts, Inc., 1998.

Hasday, Judy L. *Marie Curie: Pioneer on the Frontier of Radioactivity*. Berkeley Heights, N.J.: Enslow Publishers, Incorporated, 2004.

Heilbron, J. L. *Ernest Rutherford and the Explosion of Atoms*. New York: Oxford University Press, 2003.

Pasachoff, Naomi. *Marie Curie and the Science of Radioactivity*. New York: Oxford University Press, 1996.

Pasachoff, Naomi. *Niels Bohr: Physicist and Humanitarian*. Berkeley Heights, N.J.: Enslow Publishers, Inc., 2003.

Richardson, Hazel. *How to Split the Atom*. Danbury, Conn.: Franklin Watts Inc., 2001.

Internet Addresses

Ernest Rutherford—Biography
http://www.nobel.se/chemistry/laureates/1908/rutherford-bio.html

Ernest Rutherford—Scientist Supreme
http://www.rutherford.org.nz

A Science Odyssey: You Try It: Atom Builder
http://www.pbs.org/wgbh/aso/tryit/atom/

Index